BOTSWANA
The Insider's Guide

AUTHOR'S NOTE	7	The Trans-Kalahari Highway	64
WELCOME TO BOTSWANA	8	The Shakawe Route	66
Introduction	10	Botswana country map	69
Something old, something new	12	Gaborone town plan	70
		Maun town plan	71
FROM DUNG TO DIAMONDS	18	Okavango Delta & Moremi map	72
Fact file	20	Chobe, Savuti & the Pans map	73
Eco-tourism – The way forward	26	The Kasane–Nata Route	76
A history of peace	30	The Royal Route via Serowe	80
		Maun Town	82
BE ENTICED	34		
Okavango options	36	OF DESERT AND DELTA	86
The best of the rest	42		
Spring	48	ON SAFARI	92
Summer	50	Unique and diverse	94
Autumn	52	Wildlife highlights	96
Winter	54	The Okavango Delta & Moremi	98
		Chobe National Park	102
EN ROUTE	56	The Makgadikgadi Pans	104
Gabs City	58	The Tuli Block	106
Gabs–Francistown Route	62		

PAGES 1–3: The peace and tranquility of a *mokoro* ride in the Jao Concession.
ABOVE: Sunset over the Makgadikgadi Pans.

Lodge to lodge	108
Food for thought	116
The overland experience	117
For the adventurous	120
Be guided	122

WILDLIFE WONDERS 128

Birdlife	130
Animal portraits	134
Predators	138
The plains game	140
Plants & trees	146
Delta Blues	148
Science & conservation at work	150

OUT OF THE WAY 152

ART FOR ALL 156

Baskets of Botswana	162

THE LIFE AND SOUL 164

The people	166
More modern	168
A culture of ceremony	172
So to speak	176

MYTH AND MYSTERY 178

Boboko Jwa Kwena	180
The stars above	181

TRAVEL DIRECTORY 182

Travel advisory	183
Contact details	186

INDEX 189

GLOSSARY 192

CONTENTS

Author's note

I am incredibly fortunate and privileged, as for more than a decade now I have been able to call the magnificent country of Botswana a second home. To call a place home means, by definition, that you have family there. This book is dedicated to the remarkable 'family' with whom I have lived and worked at Nxamaseri, without doubt my favourite place in Botswana: Person Mothanka, Intshupeleng Letsatsi, Phuraki Ngoro, Tiny Sebadietla, Len and Gladys Samaje and Adam Kapinga. They have shared their wisdom and their lives with me. Thanks also to PJ Bestelink and Chris Kruger, for it was they who so selflessly fostered my dreams of a life in the wild. My wish is that this book in some way reflects my deep passion for, and commitment to, Botswana.

It has been with the assistance and support of others that I have been able to complete this project. My thanks and heartfelt gratitude go to them: Sharon McCallum and Karen Ross for assisting with the research, Oliver Souchon from Sanctuary Lodges, Norman Galli from Kwando Safaris, Mike Penman and Angie Bunyard from Wild Lifestyles, Bernie Esterhuizen and Keesi Sefofu from Desert and Delta Safaris, Bruce Simpson, Keith Vincent and Hennie Rawlinson from Okavango Wilderness Safaris, Stuart Mackay from Mack Air, Peter and Pauline Perlstein from Okavango Helicopters, Alison Morphet and Peet le Roux from Mashatu Game Reserve, Steve Rufus from Limpopo Valley Horse Safaris, The Management at Nata Lodge, Eben and Agnes van Heerden from Kalahari Arms Hotel, Ralph Bathfield from Unchartered Africa, PJ and Barney Bestelink from Okavango Horse Safaris, Peter Holbrow from Holbrow Hunting Safaris, Ian and Gwithie Kirby and Puso and Maddie Kirby from Mokolodi Nature Reserve, Judy de Beer from Camp Itumela, David and Taryn Dugmore from Meno a Kwena, and Adrian Dandridge, Anthony Michler, Carol Walton and Toon Meganck. Thanks especially to Suzy Lumsden for her immense generosity and considerable friendship. In the production of this book, thanks to Dominique le Roux and Bev Campbell for their belief and inspiration, and to Alison Day and the rest of the production team at Struik Publishers for their creativity and hard work.

And, to Corlé, for her invaluable assistance, and for bringing such happiness and love with her.

To travel with Ian as your guide or receive advice on travel in southern and East Africa, you can contact him at:
INVENT AFRICA
Tel: +27-21-6856219
email: info@inventafrica.com
Website: www.inventafrica.com

During winter, the elephants that live along the Linyanti River have a routine to their drinking habits. By mid-morning they begin appearing from the mopane woodland in numbers, and by late afternoon most have returned there to continue feeding.

welcome to BOTSWANA

Botswana's story is one of immense success. Some say it is unrivalled in Africa. In fact, so successful has the social, political and economic development been that you will often hear the country referred to as the 'Switzerland of Africa'.

Introduction

The numerous large construction sites to be seen around Gaborone are the tell-tale signs of boom times in the capital city.

Remember that, in the 1970s, Botswana was ranked as one of the **world's poorest countries** with a GDP per capita below US$ 200 and no economy to speak of, other than a fledgling beef industry that survived only because of European subsidies. Educational facilities were minimal, with less than two percent of the population having completed primary school, only a few thousand pupils attending secondary school and fewer than 100 students enrolled in university courses, and all of these outside the country. No urban settlements were large enough or even remotely sufficiently developed to warrant city status. The country played no role in either regional or continental politics, and, almost unbelievably, there was only a single 12-kilometre-long paved road in the country.

So much has changed since then. Just consider these facts: over the last two decades the economy has achieved the world's **highest average annual growth rate** and today the GDP per capita is in excess of US$3 500, while the national coffers hold over US$6 billion in foreign reserves. With a total population of just over 1.5 million people, Botswana has primary school enrolment approaching 350 000 pupils, and secondary school over 150 000. Botswana has its own university with various satellite campuses around the country teaching over 15 000 students. There are now in excess of 6 500 kilometres of paved road, and the capital Gaborone is a thriving metropolitan area and the continent's fastest-growing city. Part of the reward for its incredible transformation is that Botswana has since become a respected and stable member of various multilateral organisations, both local and international.

The changes are not all coincidence or luck, as some sceptics would have it. A number of factors have contributed to these achievements. The historical settlement of Botswana occurred largely because of people fleeing conflicts elsewhere, and so, generally speaking, the **populace is a peace-loving one** with no history of civil war or other serious internal conflict. Unlike much of Africa, Botswana was never fully colonised and so avoided a divisive struggle for independence. They are a relatively **homogeneous nation**, as almost 60 percent of the people belong to one of the Tswana groups and nearly all speak Setswana, the national language. As a result there is a patriotic unity, with the vast majority viewing themselves first and foremost as Botswanan citizens, before considering the ethnic group to which they belong.

Above all, Botswana has been blessed with **great leaders**, men who have guided the nation and its people with vision and commitment. While the **discovery of diamonds** shortly after independence was undoubtedly the major catalyst for the growth, prosperity has been brought about because of the wise manner in which the mining revenues have been handled. There are many examples, both in Africa and worldwide, where countries blessed with a far greater supply of natural resources have not achieved even remotely what this country has. Following a proud tradition of strong leadership established in prior periods by customary chiefs, the more recent political leaders have for the most part shunned the inflammatory and flamboyant style seen in so many other newly-declared states. **Sir Seretse Khama**, the first president and by all accounts a true statesman, set the example. His foresight, dedication and astuteness were followed by his successor, **Dr Ketumile Masire**, and are being built on by the incumbent president, **Festus Mogae**.

But the picture is not all rosy, as with the successes have come **new challenges** for the future. Although the diamond-based economic boom has had far-reaching benefits, the general economy cannot thrive if it remains dependent on this **single commodity** alone. Africa is littered with single-product economies gone bust. To avoid this, secondary and tertiary economic activities need to be promoted, and, because the local economy is comparatively small, these should ideally be export based. This very necessary **diversification** will also help meet what will probably be the country's most demanding responsibility – that of fulfilling the considerable **expectations of the younger generations**. Having been raised and educated on the proceeds of the diamond industry, they now want to participate in Botswana's good fortune. As with the youth in much of Africa, a life based around tradition and in a rural setting has little appeal. For them a career and an improved standard of living with modern conveniences, preferably within an urban community, have become the ambition.

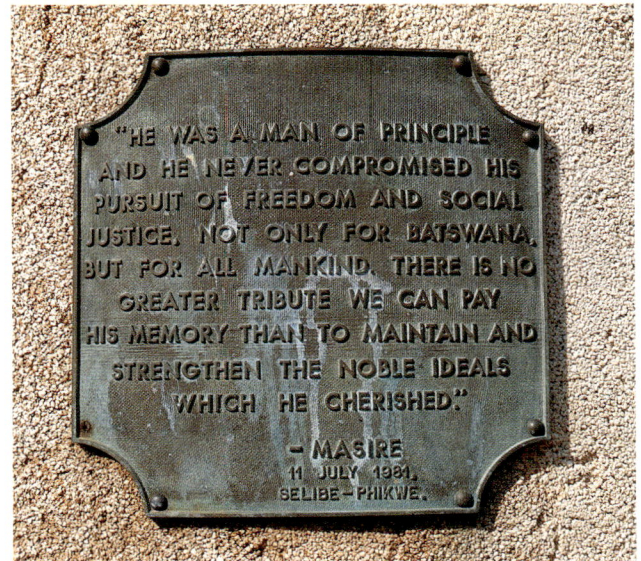

Sir Seretse Khama was a visionary leader – this plaque honouring him appears in the public garden at Jwaneng.

Although some still don't believe it, the country's major asset is its almost **unparalleled wildlife resources** and the selection of near pristine environments it contains. The tourism industry, based mainly on eco-tourism, is currently providing a substantial boost to the northern regions of the country in particular. While the diamond and other mineral reserves are in decline, sustainable eco-tourism could exist in perpetuity. The challenge is to ensure the long-term protection of Botswana's natural resources by promoting sustainable policies.

The country has also not escaped the continent-wide **HIV and AIDS pandemic**. It is of major concern that most surveys indicate over 30 percent of the population is infected, giving the country one of the highest infection rates worldwide. Fortunately, the political will and the financial resources to tackle the problem are available. Botswana has introduced the Vision 2016 campaign, which is aiming to achieve an AIDS-free Botswana by this date.

But, in spite of these demands, there is much hope for the future of the country. **Ian Khama**, who is the current vice president and son of Sir Seretse Khama, is expected to become the next president in the 2004 elections. He is seen as a bold and inspiring man, who will be able to lead the nation into the next era.

Welcome to Botswana or, as the locals say, *'Goroga sentle mo Botswana'*. I just love this country, and I sincerely hope and trust you will.

Travelling in Botswana brings many joys. One that is always particularly pleasing is the visibility of the country's success. The rewards are on display, often highlighted in both urban and rural settings, as the old and traditional are juxtaposed with the new and modern. Whether it be the accommodation of the House of Chiefs in parliament, the maintaining of the strength of the *kgotla* (where traditional judicial proceedings are conducted) system in rural areas, or the construction of high-rise buildings alongside mud huts, the total acceptance of both aspects as an integral part of daily life is a crucial component of Botswana's stability.

TOP: A Herero woman from Sehitwa on her cellphone. This advance in technology has spread to many rural areas in Botswana.
MIDDLE LEFT: A man brings freshly cut reeds from the Delta to rewall his village home.
ABOVE: Donkeys are a common sight on the streets of Maun.
LEFT: For this rural homeowner — with his humble home and state-of-the art toilet — it's obviously a question of priorities.

Something old, something new

A common sight in Botswana's smaller towns is a traditional mud hut and a more modern dwelling built alongside each other on the same property.

ABOVE: A sign of the times: recently installed telephone booths have been placed in most of the rural towns in order to compete with cellphones.
OPPOSITE: Satellite dishes are a sure sign of improving living standards.

A radio mast towers above traditional mud and thatch dwellings in Nata.

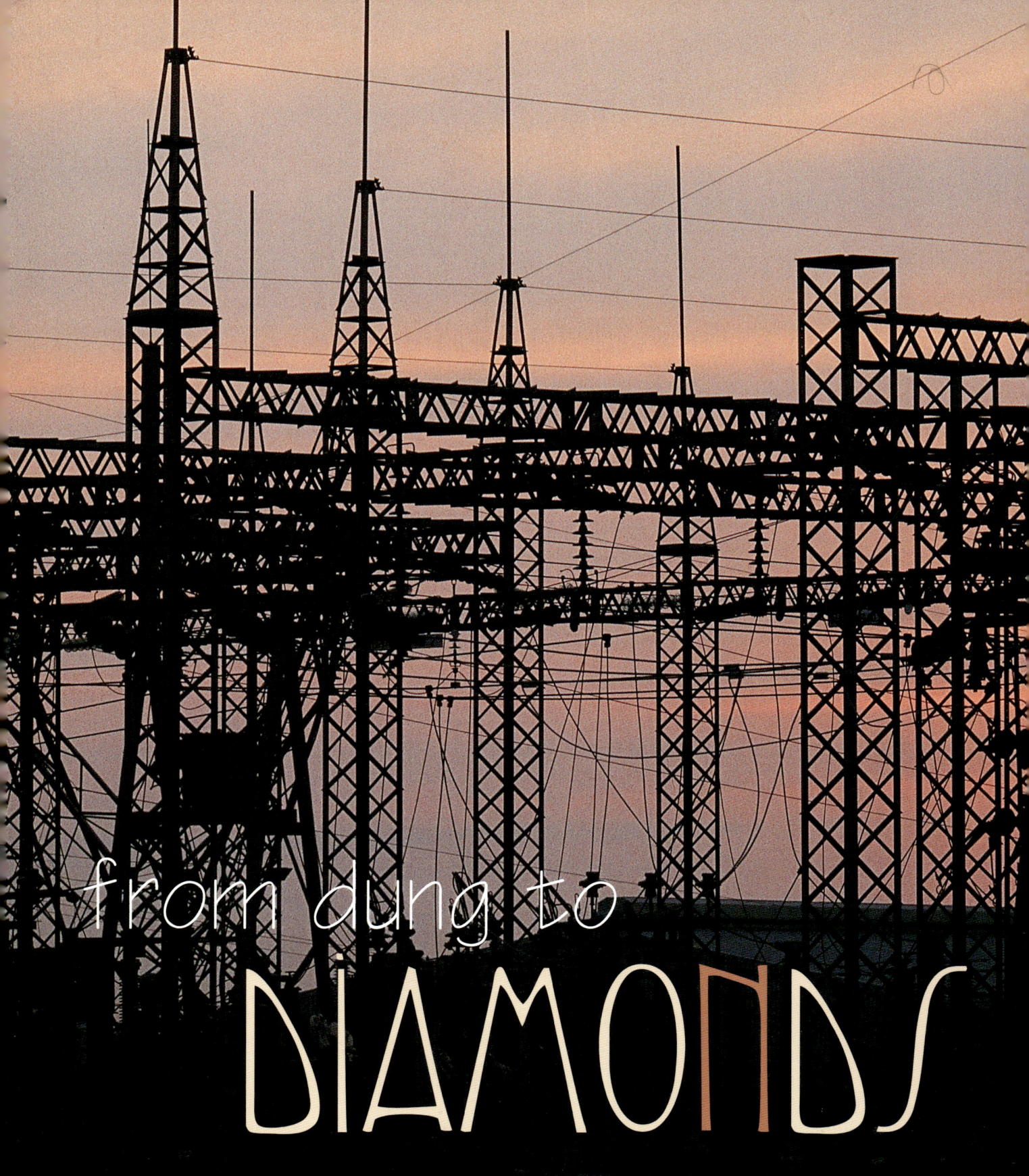

Botswana's political stability and success have been fuelled by rapid economic and social development. Ranked as one of the world's poorest countries at independence in 1966, with the cattle industry its only viable and productive sector, it has become a middle-income country that is the world's leading producer of gem-quality diamonds.

FACT FILE

Area	581 730 square kilometres
Population	1.68 million (2001 census)
Density	2.9 people per square kilometre
Population growth rate	2.4 percent
Urban population	49.4 percent
Capital city	Gaborone
Principal towns	Francistown, Selebi-Phikwe, Molepolole, Kanye and Serowe
Coastline	Landlocked
Nationally protected areas	17 percent of the country
Wildlife management areas	22 percent of the country
Independence	1966
National day	30 September
Official language	English
National language	Setswana
Currency	Pula (100 thebe = one Pula)
Economic growth rate	7.0 percent (average over five yrs)
Annual GDP	US$ 5.28 billion (2001)
GNI per capita	US$ 3 650.00 (2001)

▶▶ The country is called Botswana because almost 60 percent of its inhabitants are **Setswana- (or Tswana-) speakers**. Botswana means 'the land of the Tswana'. The language is called Setswana and the citizens are known as Batswana.

▶▶ **The Republic of Botswana** is a multi-party democracy with legislative power vested in a single chamber of parliament. This body, the **National Assembly**, has a total of 44 members, 40 of whom are elected directly by the voting population in elections that are held every five years. The members of the National Assembly elect the remaining four from a list submitted by the president. In addition, the Attorney General and the Speaker of the House sit in the National Assembly.

▶▶ **Executive power** lies with the president of Botswana who appoints a vice president and cabinet. The Presidency is limited to two five-year terms in office.

▶▶ **The House of Chiefs** is an advisory body that acts as a support to the National Assembly, particularly on issues relating to the rural areas and traditional life. This body has 15 members, comprising the eight chiefs from the principal groups within Botswana and seven who are in turn elected by these members.

▶▶ **Diamonds** are the major component of the economy, contributing almost 70 percent of foreign earnings and approximately 32 percent of GDP. Other metals and minerals mined in the country include copper, nickel, coal, cobalt, soda ash and gold.

▶▶ **Industry** comprises almost 20 percent of GDP, with textiles, food and beverage processing, light engineering and leather and related craft production forming the major components of this sector.

▶▶ **Agricultural production**, primarily of beef, used to comprise over 45 percent of GDP at independence in 1966, but this has now fallen below four percent. The sector is, however, the country's largest employer as it provides some source of income for almost 80 percent of the population. The country receives subsidies from the European Union for its beef, which goes mainly to the United Kingdom, Norway, Denmark, Italy and Greece. The national herd consists of almost 3 million cattle.

▶▶ **Tourism** is the fastest-growing sector of the economy and the one that supports the less developed northern and western regions of the country. Although its contribution to GDP is still below 20 percent, it is a large employer, the second-largest foreign exchange earner, and has been responsible for creating enormous knock-on benefits to the secondary economy. This sector offers great potential for Botswana in the future.

▶▶ **Land tenure** falls into three broad categories: communal or tribal land comprises 71 percent of the country, State land (which includes all national parks and reserves) 23 percent, and freehold land occupies six percent, mostly in the east and around Gaborone, Francistown and Ghanzi. All citizens living in communal areas are entitled to land free of charge for residential, agricultural and commercial purposes.

▶▶ In general, **population density** increases from west to east, with almost 80 percent of the population

There are three large open-cast diamond mines: Jwaneng, Orapa and Letlhakane, which together produce over 22 percent of the world's gem-quality diamonds.

living in the eastern corridor from Francistown to Gaborone and their surrounding towns. While the average density is just over 2.6 people per square kilometre, in parts of the central regions it is under 0.5 persons per square kilometre, and as high as 450 in the cities and towns of the east and south.

▶▶ **Education** is free and, although strongly encouraged, is not compulsory. There are over 730 primary schools and 270 secondary schools, which provide 12 years of education and the highest teacher-pupil ratio in Africa. The country has over 50 colleges and technical education facilities for school-leavers, and one university. The literacy rate is approximately 73 percent.

▶▶ **The legal system** is based on Roman-Dutch and customary law. It is administered through a number of regional magistrates' courts operating under the High Court and a Court of Appeal. Customary Courts are recognised, and they deal with minor issues within rural communities. The judiciary is viewed as being fully independent of the State, and the country's ultimate penalty is that of death by hanging.

▶▶ Botswana was a founder member of the **Southern African Development Community** (SADC) – the secretariat remains in Gaborone – and the country is also a member of the United Nations, the African Union, the Commonwealth, the Non-Aligned Movement, the Southern African Customs Union and the World Trade Organisation.

▶▶ **The national flag** comprises a simple grid pattern with the colours blue, black and white. Blue, which represents rain and water, dominates the flag, as it is a symbol of the prosperity this precious natural element brings to the country. The black and white stripes are symbolic of the harmony amongst the various race groups. The zebra, which appears on the coat of arms, is the country's national animal. Botswana has no national bird or flower.

Are diamonds forever?

Diamonds have earned Botswana its wealth and, along with this, the status of being recognised as one of the world's most successful economies. The first kimberlite pipes were discovered in 1967 at **Orapa** and production commenced in 1971. Two other major mines followed: **Letlhakane** in 1977 and **Jwaneng**, which produces the most carats, in 1982. Presently there are more than 200 kimberlite pipes at 12 different fields, and most mining is open-pit or at a shallow level, making for some of the lowest-cost mining worldwide. All three diamond mines are operated by **DEBSWANA**, which is a 50-50 partnership between the Botswana Government and De Beers of South Africa. With just over 22 percent of world production, Botswana is the leading producer of gem-quality stones in the world. Over 28 million carats were produced last year.

However, the substantial impact that diamonds have had on Botswana's success has resulted in the government becoming overly dependent on this single-source revenue. Contrary to the popular ads, diamonds are not forever, and the biggest challenge facing the country and its leaders is to diversify the economic base, broaden the sources of government revenue and promote sectors that provide substantial job creation and spread wealth more evenly.

While the diamond industry is the largest foreign exchange earner and contributes a large percentage of GDP, it employs relatively few people and does not offer a solid platform on which to base future growth and development. At present values, **reserves** are forecast to last only another 35 years. Fortunately, political leaders and entrepreneurs are aware of this, and they have been attempting to attract manufacturing and related secondary and tertiary industries to the country. Sectors that have been targeted include light engineering, food and beverage processing and textiles.

Good governance

In the 2003/04 **Competitiveness Report** conducted by the **World Economic Forum** (WEF), Botswana was ranked first amongst all African countries surveyed. The study looked at issues such as the rule of law, impressions of corruption and the enforcement of contracts for an overall assessment of competitiveness and prospects for economic growth. Generally, the country has always had an excellent reputation in this regard, which has been one of the major factors in its overall success.

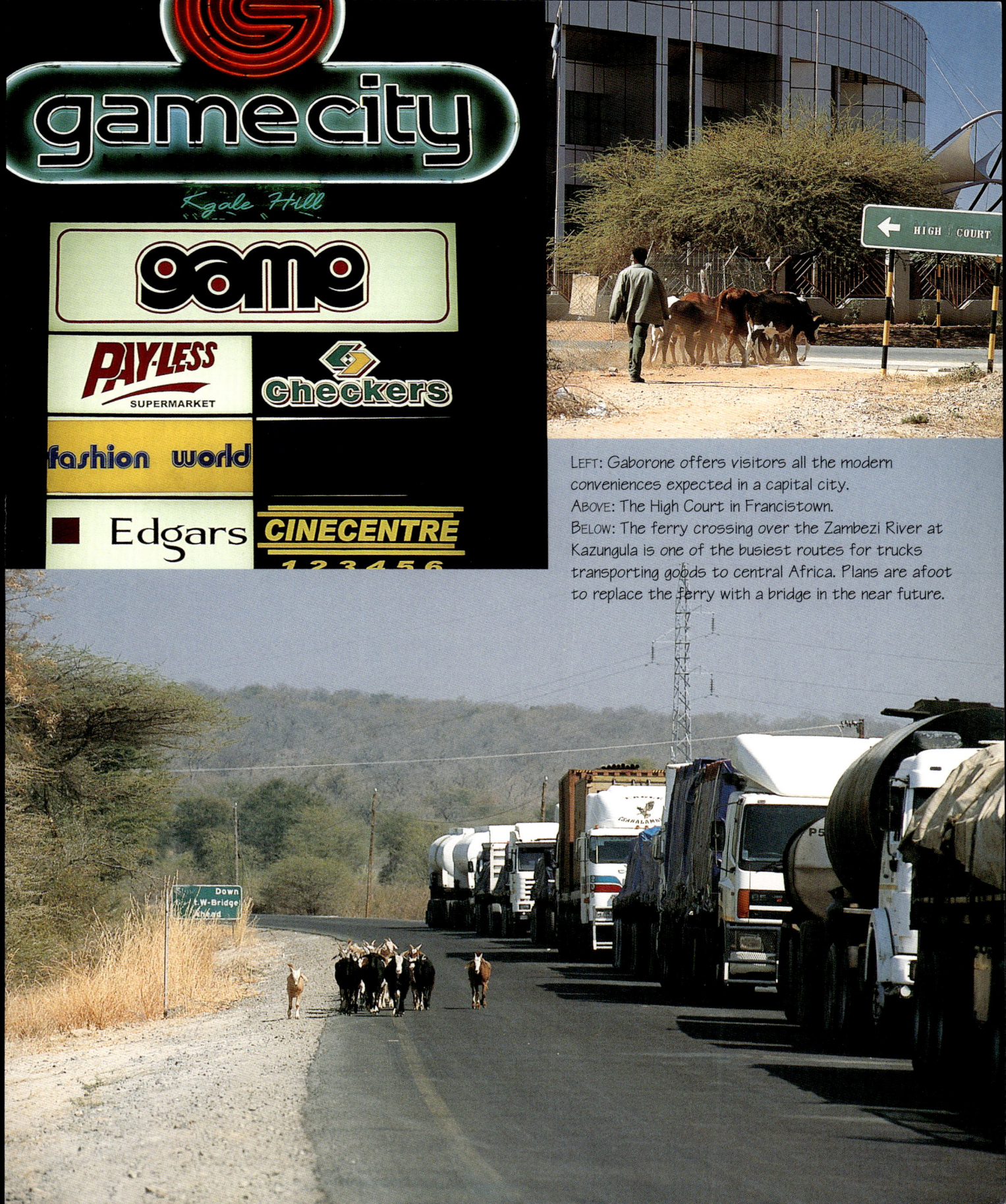

LEFT: Gaborone offers visitors all the modern conveniences expected in a capital city.
ABOVE: The High Court in Francistown.
BELOW: The ferry crossing over the Zambezi River at Kazungula is one of the busiest routes for trucks transporting goods to central Africa. Plans are afoot to replace the ferry with a bridge in the near future.

The old and traditional appear juxtaposed with the new and modern – the acceptance of both aspects as an integral part of daily life is a crucial component of Botswana's stability.

Eco-tourism
The way forward

High cost—low volume eco-tourism

Although most of Botswana is classified as being semi-arid, the country still has a large wildlife population. These animals are mostly free-ranging, as they occur not only in the designated parks and reserves, but also within community areas and across tribal lands throughout most of the country. This feature gives the country an invaluable competitive advantage within Africa that serves as a major drawcard for safari tourists. But, because of the fragile environment, and out of a desire to avoid the more mass-market type safari experience found in parts of east and southern Africa, the country has chosen to manage its wildlife resources according to the '**high cost—low volume**' maxim. In essence, the aim is to manage the wildlife areas in a sustainable manner by attracting fewer visitors, who pay higher average prices. The result is that excessive pressure is not placed on the country's natural resources and visitors experience a more exclusive safari, and also one in pristine conditions. The **Department of Wildlife and National Parks (DWNP)**, the regional land boards and various other government agencies, enforce this principle, as it's laid out in the **Wildlife Conservation Policy**, the **National Conservation Strategy** and a number of tourism acts introduced in the early 1990s.

For the people living alongside wildlife areas, the crucial component of any successful eco-tourism policy is that empowerment of their communities takes place. In order to ensure this, the **Department of Tourism** has a division devoted to developing and expanding the concepts of eco-tourism. Their chief focus is on education, promoting the sustainable utilisation of all natural tourism resources and to encourage and facilitate the active participation of citizens in the tourism industry.

Tourism bytes

▶▶ Approximately 17 percent of the country has been set aside in national parks and game reserves, and another 22 percent has been allocated to **Wildlife Management Areas (WMAs)**. With 39 percent of its land under either national, private or community protection, Botswana ranks in the top three countries in the world for conservation.

▶▶ Prior to 1995 most of the wildlife areas were controlled as hunting concessions and were largely under-utilised. That changed with the new **Land Utilisation acts** and the subsequent boom in the photographic safari sector is what has given the tourism industry its primary boost over the last decade. It's viewed as the main growth industry for the future.

▶▶ Botswana is now ranked in the top five most popular destinations in Africa.

▶▶ The vision statement of the **Department of Tourism** says that: 'By the year 2009, we, the Department of Tourism, will have facilitated the development, diversification and promotion of sustainable tourism products, thereby positioning Botswana amongst the top ten preferred destinations in the world.'

▶▶ The Department of Tourism falls under the **Ministry of Environment, Wildlife and Tourism**, and was only created in 1994, giving an indication of how young the industry still is.

▶▶ In the latest statistical report put out by the Department of Tourism, **international tourism receipts** had grown from US$136 million in 1997 to US$313 million by 2002.

▶▶ The same report noted that there were 442 **licensed tourism enterprises** at the end of 2002, up from 202 in 1998. The number of tented camps and lodges has increased from 77 to 158, and the number of mobile safari operators from 54 to 134.

▶▶ Of the 442 tourism enterprises with licenses, 178 are citizen owned (47 in 1998), 148 are non-citizen owned (81 in 1998) and 116 are joint ventures (74 in 1998).

▶▶ The number of beds available for tourists in the country almost doubled between 1998 and 2002 to over 6 300.

▶▶ The Department of Wildlife and National Parks manages a total of 153 campsites, which can accommodate 6 438 people at any given time. In 2002 a total of 30 799 tourists visited the campsites adding P1.34 million to government revenues.

RIGHT: Kings Pool Camp in the Linyanti Concession.
BELOW: Eco-tourism has been recognised as the way forward in managing the country's wildlife resources.
BOTTOM LEFT: Viewing suricates in the Makgadikgadi Pans.
BOTTOM RIGHT: Gudikwa Village is a successful community-based eco-tourism project. Visitors to the village, which is owned and managed by the local Bushman community, get to learn about the culture, traditions and values of the country's first inhabitants.

Despite the country's economic successes, most families in the rural areas still rely on firewood as their primary source of fuel.

A history of peace

From a historical perspective, the arid Kalahari thirstland of what is now known as Botswana has been pivotal, both in prehistoric and more recent times. Because of its central position in southern Africa, people's migration from surrounding areas in order to escape ongoing conflicts and settle in the less troubled interior, has characterised its history. Recognition must also go to the leadership and vision of the country's earlier chiefs who negotiated protection for their people, thus preventing occupation and colonisation. This has given rise to a largely peace-loving nation, who, for the most part, have lived in harmony, not only with each other, but also with their neighbouring countries.

20 000 BC: Although they comprise only a small part of the population today, the area that is now Botswana was originally, for many thousands of years, inhabited by the semi-nomadic hunter-gatherer Bushman people. They are known locally as the Basarwa, and are related to the pastoralist Khoikhoi. Archaeological evidence, gathered from tools made of wood, bone and stone unearthed at Tsodilo Hills in the north-west, suggests continuous occupation by the Khoikhoi and the Bushmen from c. 17 000 BC to c. AD 1650.

AD 190–AD 450: Bantu-speaking settlers from the north began moving into surrounding territories before the first millennium was out, bringing with them an Iron Age farming culture based on the raising of cattle and cultivation of grain crops. They began migrating into present-day Botswana, slowly replacing the nomadic and pastoral Khoikhoi and Bushmen in many areas. Evidence of their influence can be found in the northern regions with the remains of small beehive-shaped grass-mat houses (c. AD 420) that were used by these farmers. There is also evidence west of the Okavango River, alongside the Khoikhoi and Bushman sites in Tsodilo Hills, of similar farming settlements. From around the same period, there is evidence of an Iron Age iron-smelting furnace, dated c. AD 190 in Tswapong Hills, near Palapye.

AD 500: During the ensuing centuries, the tendency of different chiefs and their followers to leave main groups and settle in other areas resulted in the settlement patterns of the region's modern people. The first to arrive were the Zhizo, thought to be the ancestors of the Bakalanga. They were a non-Setswana-speaking group of Bantu who came from present-day Zimbabwe and settled in the north-east, around Francistown.

1000–1300: The Toutswe, an offshoot of the Zhizo, who settled in the Palapaye region a few hundred years later, followed them, as did the Mapungubwe who settled in the Mahalapye region around 1300.

1400–1500: Most of Botswana's present-day inhabitants are Setswana-speaking and are descended from the Sotho people, who originally came from around the headwaters of the Limpopo River. During the middle of this period, the first groups to arrive were the Bakgalagadi who settled in the south and central regions. Later came the Babirwa who settled in the Bobonong area.

1600–1700: During this century three Setswana-speaking brothers split from their family group, forming the beginnings of three prominent Setswana-speaking groups of today. The Bakwena settled in the Molepolole area, the Bangwaketse in the Kanye district and the Bangwato around Serowe.

1750–1800: The Bangwato split, with Chief Khama I remaining in Serowe, while his brother Tawana moved north to establish the Batawana clan around Lake Ngami and the southern fringes of the Okavango Delta. Other non-Setswana-speaking people arrived during the late 1700s, mostly from the north. The Bayei, Mbukushu and Basubiya splintered from the Balozi Kingdom in present-day Zambia and settled the northern regions, along the Linyanti, Chobe and Okavango rivers.

1800–1835: As the ivory, cattle and slave trade spread inland from the Cape Colony and the coasts of Mozambique and Angola, the whole area experienced

Botswana has one of the proudest records of democracy in Africa, with free and fair elections held every five years. The constitution promotes respect for the rule of law and protects freedom of speech and association, and the country has a free and open press.

increasingly unsettled times. The Boer trekkers from the Transvaal were involved in various cattle and land wars with the local people, and great instability and militancy in Zululand – known as the period of the Difaqane (exodus) – forced many more groups to move into what is now Botswana, in search of land and peace. The Barolong and Balete came from the south and the Bakgatla and Batlokwa from the southeast during the early to mid 1800s. Zulu raiding parties under the control of Mzilikazi won control over large areas held by the Bangwato and Bangwaketse, forcing families deeper into the Kalahari.

1841: Christian missionaries began to establish their influence in the early 1800s, with Robert Moffat the first to arrive. David Livingstone followed in 1841, before establishing the first school in the country. From 1829 to 1892 the Tswana king of the Bakwena, Sechele, ruled around Molepolole and allied himself with British traders and missionaries, eventually being baptised by David Livingstone.

1872–1880: By the late 1870s the Bangwato, the largest Tswana nation, had taken control of Kwena under the chiefdom of Khama III, who ruled from 1872 to 1923.

1885: As a result of Boer expansionism, and to a lesser extent continuing Ndebele incursions from the northwest, Botswana came under British protection in 1885. The Berlin Conference defined the boundaries of present-day Botswana, and a British protectorate was formally declared over the area then called Bechuanaland. The administrative capital was Mafekeng, which was in the adjoining Cape Colony outside the territory's borders. At one stage the protectorate fell under the control of the Cape Colony.

1894–1895: In 1894 Cecil John Rhodes and his British South Africa Company (BSAC) motivated for the annexation of Bechuanaland. This hostile move prompted three Batswana chiefs, Sebele, Khama III and Bathoen I, to sail for Britain in 1895 to petition the government to keep their land under British protection. They were successful after the British public sided with them, but one condition was given: that the BSAC be entitled to build a railway line to then southern Rhodesia (now Zimbabwe) through their lands.

1896: Chief Sekgoma, head of the Batawana, ceded Ghanzi to the British government to allow white settlement to take place within the central regions around the town of Ghanzi. In return the British gave sovereignty of Ngamiland to the Batawana.

1900: The last of the present-day Botswanan groups to settle in the country were the Mbanderu and the Baherero, who fled the German occupation of what is now Namibia in the early 1900s and established their livestock-based lifestyle along the western and southern reaches of the Okavango.

1910: Since the three chiefs (of the Bakwena, Bangwaketse and Bangwato) had been promised by the British, Bechuanaland was excluded from the country established with the formation of the Union of South Africa in 1910.

1923: Khama III was one of the chiefs involved in the agreement resulting in the protectorate. Under his rule, peace and stability returned to the land and his people, the Bangwato, became a leading force in Bechuanaland. On his death in 1923 he was succeeded by his son, Sekgoma, who died two years later. As Sekgoma's eldest son, Seretse, was still only a child, his older half-brother, Tshekedi, ruled in his place.

1948: It was during this period that Seretse travelled to England for his schooling and tertiary education, and it was there that he met and married Ruth Williams, a white woman, in 1948. The marriage split his people back home: Tshekedi, a strict traditionalist, was particularly strongly opposed to the inter-racial union. Because of the dispute, the British banned both Khama and Tshekedi from Botswanan tribal lands.

1956: Khama was eventually allowed to return with his wife in 1956, but only as a private citizen, as he had been persuaded to renounce his claim to the Bangwato chieftainship.

1961: From 1952, Seretse's supporters began to organise themselves politically. After his return he became a member of both the executive and legislative councils formed in 1961 in terms of the new Bechuanaland constitution, which had been drawn up a year earlier.

1962: Seretse Khama and Ketumile Masire formed the moderate Bechuanaland Democratic Party (now the Botswana Democratic Party or BPD).

1965–1966: The protectorate was granted internal self government in 1965 and on 30 September 1966 the country was granted full independence. The Republic of Botswana came into being, with Seretse Khama its first president, and Gaborone as the administrative capital. Seretse Khama received a British knighthood shortly thereafter.

1967–1974: Diamonds were discovered at Orapa, followed by later discoveries at Jwaneng and Lethlakane. This was the major factor in the country achieving economic growth and independence from South Africa, and from 1969 onwards Botswana began to play a significant role in international politics as a non-racial liberal country. In 1974 the copper-nickel mine at Selebi-Pikwe became operational, providing a further boost to the economy of the fledgling democracy.

1975–1976: The Bank of Botswana was instituted in 1975, and in 1976 Botswana's own currency, the Pula, replaced the South African currency previously in use.

1980: Sir Seretse Khama died in 1980 and was succeeded by his deputy, Ketumile Masire. During the 1980s, and up until the present day, the economy continued to expand and improve as a result of revenue from the diamond mines and beef exports, and more recently from the growth of the tourist industry.

1985: During the 1980s and 1990s South Africa was involved in ongoing internal conflict, and between 1984 and 1990 Botswana suffered at the hands of the South African army, because of guerrilla fighters seeking refuge in the country. In 1985, 12 people were killed during a South African military raid into Gaborone.

1986: Twenty years after independence, Gaborone attained city status.

1998–present: Ketumile Masire retired as president in 1998 and was succeeded by the vice president Festus Mogae, after he won the election in October 1999. Ian Khama, the son of Sir Seretse Khama, is the current vice president. The next election is due in October 2004.

Tin cans are still used in the rural towns and villages as building material. There are cost benefits, and houses built in this manner are said to stay cooler during the summer months.

be ENTICED

Choosing a travel destination is all about the excitement of exploration and opening the mind and soul to new experiences. But it is also about returning to favourite haunts that ring with memories. And, for most, so much the better if the destination is safe and reliable. Botswana has a world of thrilling options to offer the first-time traveller and those who return time and again.

Mekoro, or dugout canoes, were traditionally made from a variety of hardwood trees such as African ebony and Rhodesian teak. As they have an average life of no more than three to five years, and because of the massive growth in tourism, they are now made from fibreglass moulds in order to spare the trees.

Okavango options

TRAVEL IN DECEMBER Contrary to conventional marketing wisdom, the Delta in December is a stunning place to be, especially for those seeking a more secluded safari. Stormy skies cast a spectacular shadow over the flush of green brought on by the first rains, and it also happens to be the calving season for many of the plains game species – adding an air of *joie de vivre* to your game drives.

UNDER THE NIGHT SKIES Sleeping under the stars is on everyone's wish list, so why not do it with the sound of lion and hyena in the background? For the romantics, choose the luxury of crisp cotton and flowing mosquito nets in the Jao Concession, or opt for the rustic charm of camping out on a *mokoro* (a traditional dugout canoe) trail from Chief's Island. There are many other alternatives, but, whatever your choice, make doubly sure it is with a recognised operator.

HORSEBACK SAFARI Cantering amongst herds of zebra and wildebeest across open floodplains is possibly the most exhilarating of all safari experiences. Mount up and become one with the wildlife while riding out of either Kujwana or Macatoo.

A BIRDER'S PARADISE Botswana is not only big game country. Anytime from September to March you should be able to spot most of the bird specials, including Pel's fishing owl, African skimmers, slaty egret and wattled cranes. For the maximum species count, try a water camp in the Panhandle and a game camp in the Delta or Chobe/Linyanti/Kwando system.

ELEPHANT BACK SAFARI For the well-heeled, staying for three to five nights at Abu Camp not only buys you bragging rights, but also the most stylish safari of all and an incredible intimacy with the elephants. With a little luck you may also get to chew Cuban cigars with safari operator Randall Moore and hear the fireside version of his inspiring life and times with the herd.

A TIGER ON A FLY This is possibly the most thrilling of all freshwater fishing experiences. For the best tiger fishing, head for Nxamaseri Lodge or Drotsky's Cabins in the Panhandle during the annual catfish runs, which occur anytime from August through to November. And, remember, you should always catch and release.

A MOKORO TRAIL Without doubt the most traditional and tranquil way to undertake a safari in the Okavango. Sit back, relax and let the wilderness wash over you as you get poled about the waterways in a dugout canoe. Do it in comfort on the Xigera Trail, or rough it a little from Oddballs or Guma Lagoon Camp.

RHINO AT MOMBO Indiscriminate hunting and commercial poaching have taken their toll on the country's rhino populations, but now, after almost two decades of being extinct in the wild, some have been returned to the Okavango. Mombo Camp, one of Africa's foremost wildlife destinations, is the best place to see them.

FLIGHTS OF FANCY Spoil yourself by flying with Peter and Pauline Perlstein of Okavango Helicopters. Whether you opt for a short Delta game-viewing flight, an inter-camp transfer or to spend time out on a picnic stopover, a helicopter flight over the Delta is an absolute thrill. Period enthusiasts can don goggles, helmet and scarf and take a flight back in time with Peter aboard his Tiger Moth biplane.

THE PANHANDLE IN AUTUMN You can experience the cool, crystal waters in the upper reaches of the Okavango River at their clearest, when the flood waters are at their peak. The autumn colours are picture perfect and the mild temperatures make this the most comfortable time to be here.

OPPOSITE TOP LEFT & RIGHT: Most camps have raised decking from which to view animals.
OPPOSITE MIDDLE LEFT: The floodplains of Vumbura.
OPPOSITE MIDDLE & BOTTOM: What everyone comes to see.

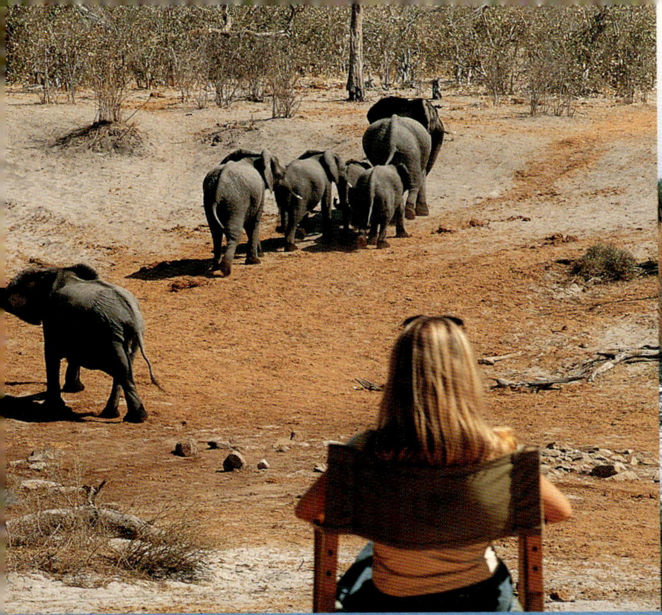

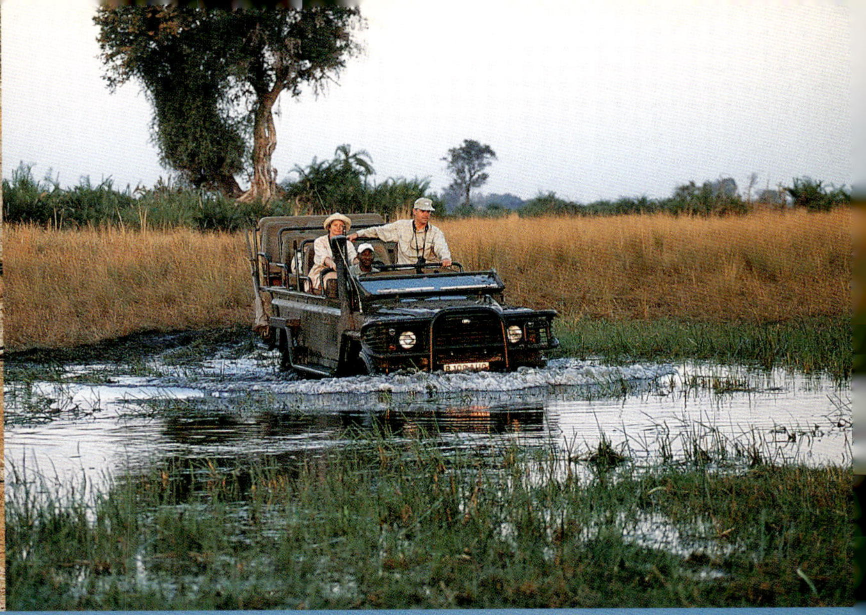

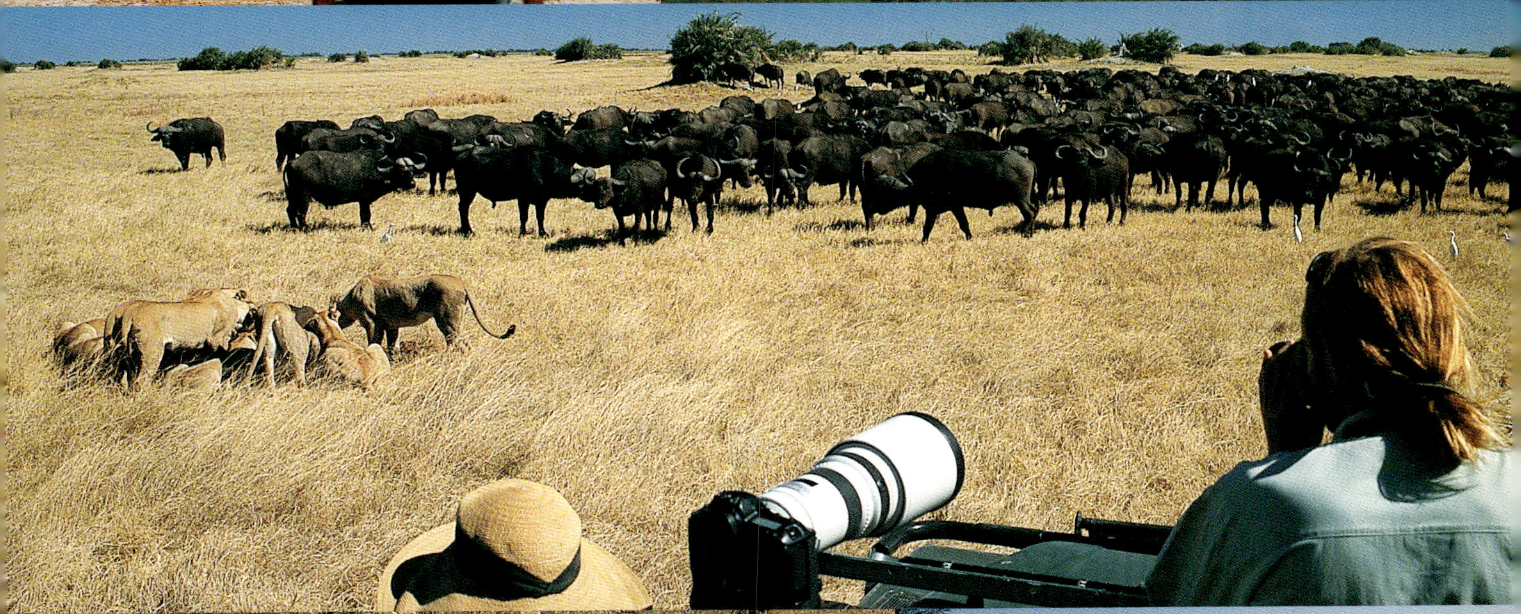

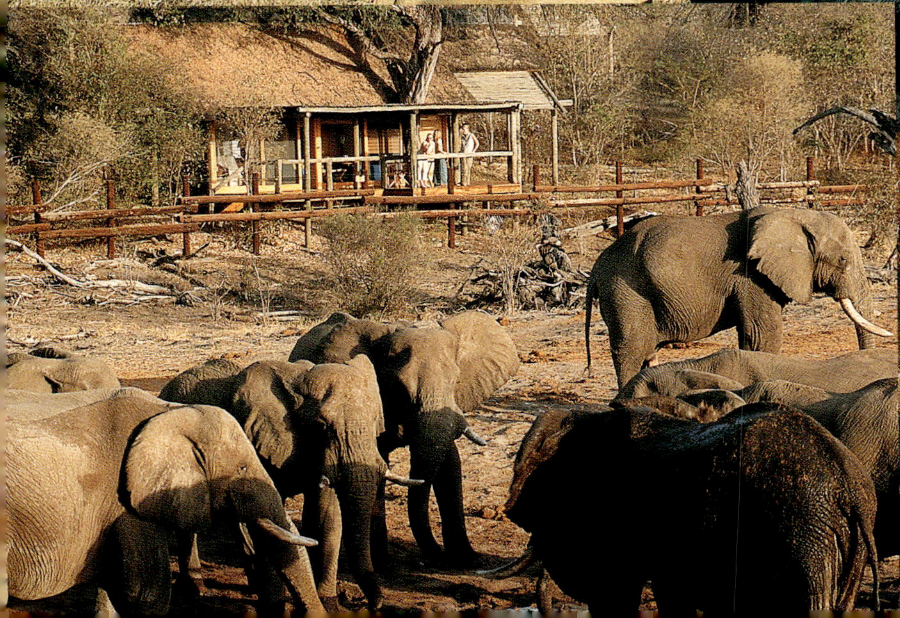

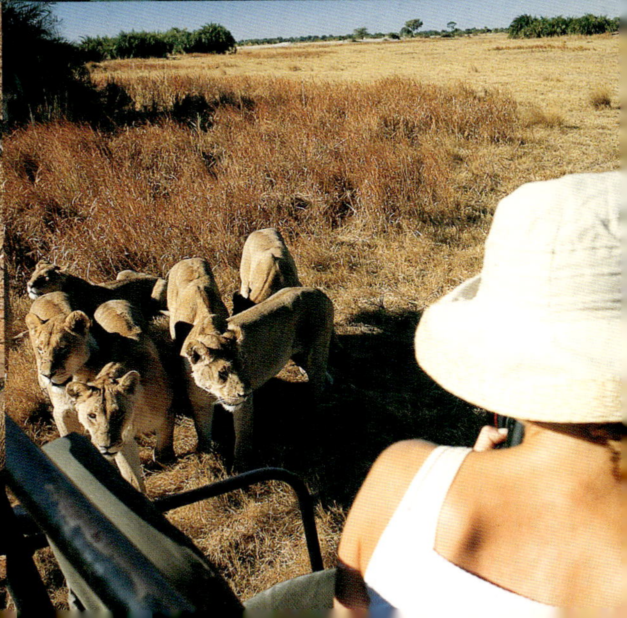

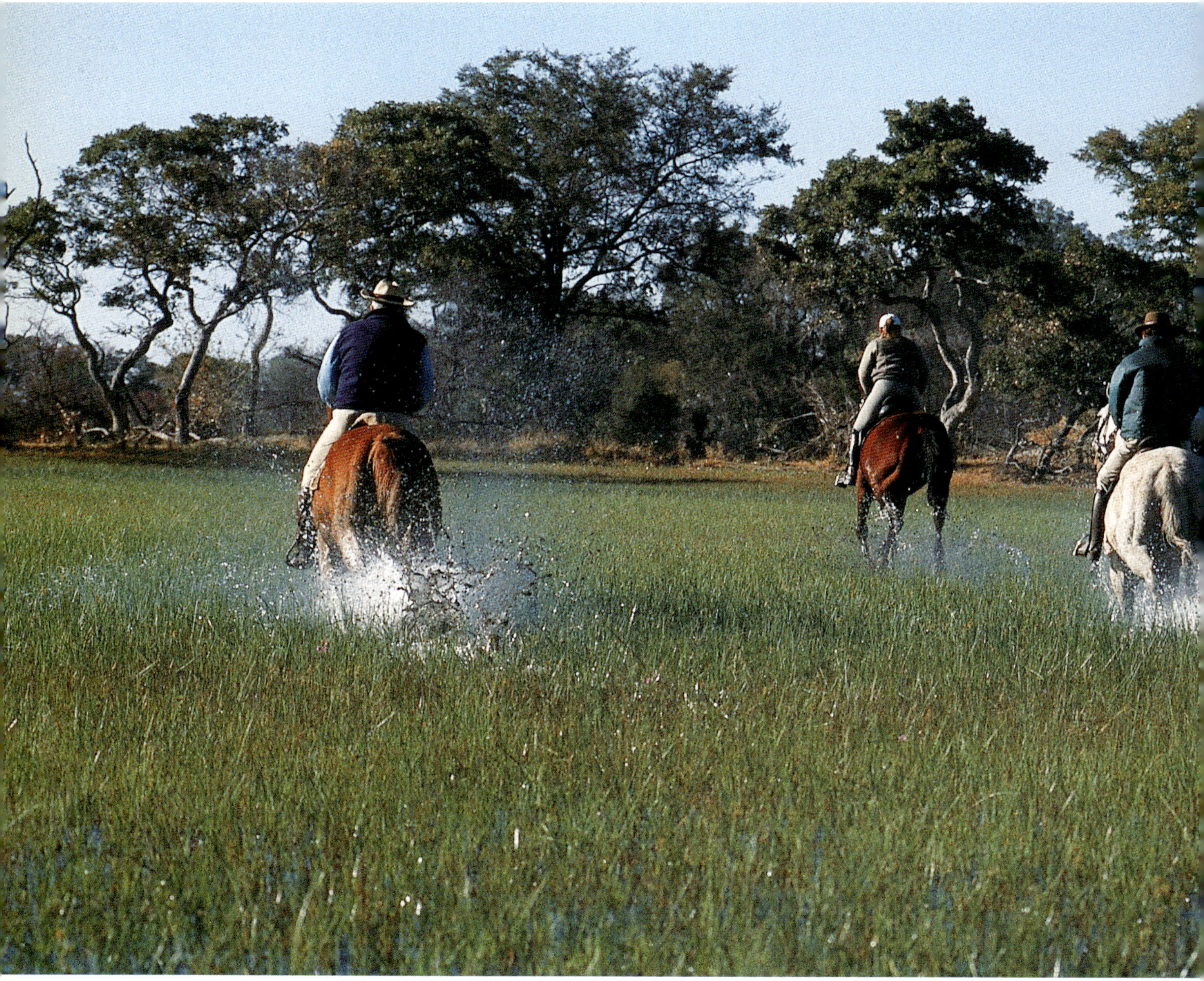

PJ and Barney Bestelink of Okavango Horse Safaris lead a group of riders on a floodplain canter. Participants must know how to ride before joining a horseback safari in the Okavango.

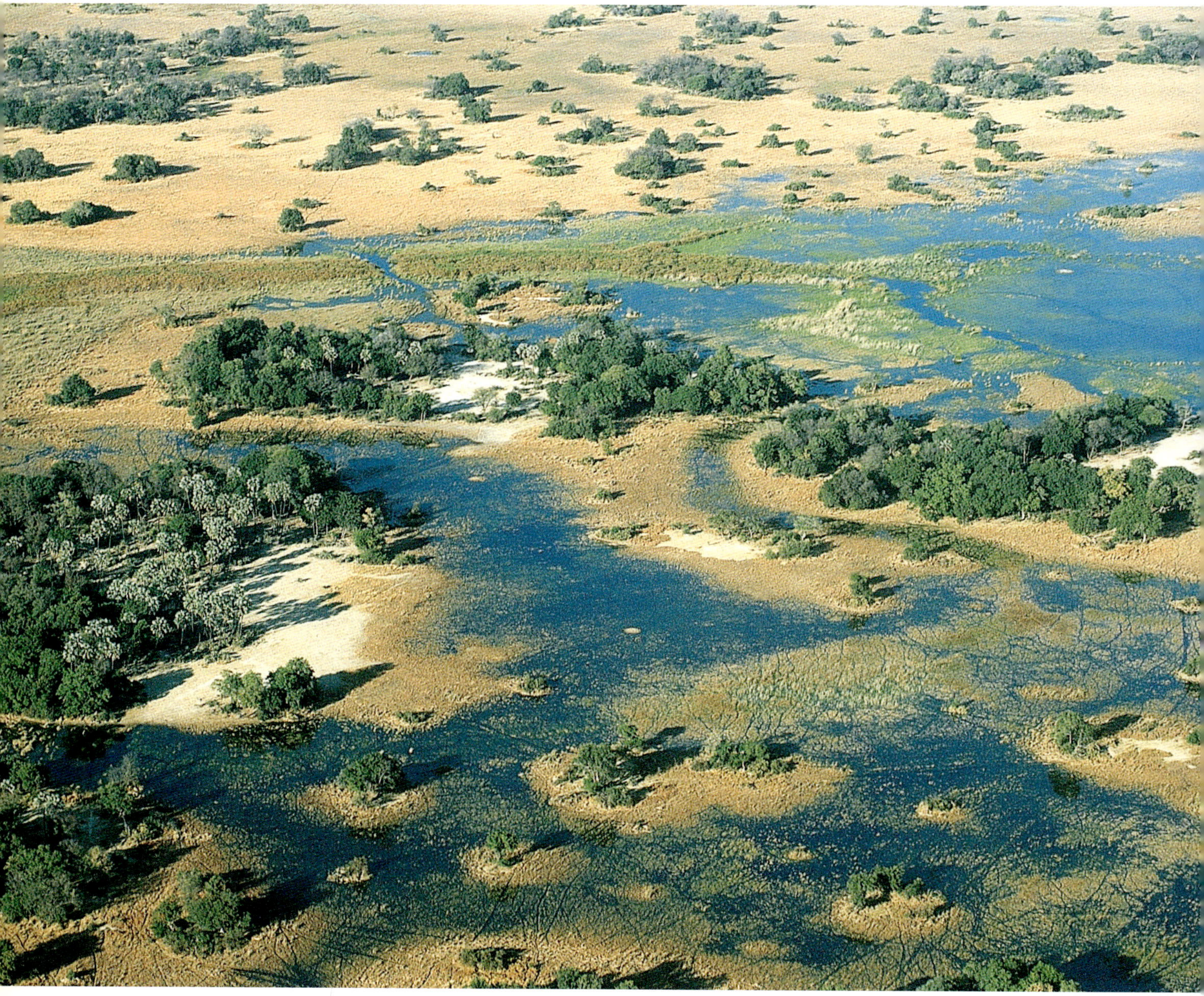

OPPOSITE: Okavango from the air a typical mosaic of islands, channels and floodplains.
ABOVE: An evening campfire is always one of the joys of being on safari.

The best of the rest

THE WOODPILE HIDE AT SAVUTI BUSH CAMP For elephant lovers in particular, this must rank as one of the most awesome wildlife experiences ever. Spend as much time as you can in the fortified hide overlooking a water hole, where you'll be surrounded by hundreds of elephants, as they jostle for drinking rights.

KWANDO Tucked away in the far north, along the border with Namibia, this concession is no longer Botswana's best-kept wildlife secret. Blessed with an extraordinary mix of terrain, it has become well known for its reliable wild dog sightings, and is one of the very best areas to see the rare roan and sable antelope.

THE TULI BLOCK Because of its proximity, Tuli has long been a favourite with South Africans and the residents of Gaborone. The privately-owned Mashatu Game Reserve offers its guests an exciting choice of horseback rides, mountain-bike trails and cultural excursions, all amongst big game and in rugged scenery that is so different from anywhere else in Botswana.

TSODILO HILLS These three sacred hills in the far north-west house one of Africa's richest collections of Bushman rock art. The most rewarding way to explore them is to spend a night or two in their embrace. After a recent upgrade to the connecting road, Tsodilo is now far more accessible.

MAKGADIKGADI PANS AT FULL MOON Explore the planet's largest salt pans on quad-bikes from Jack's Camp or Planet Baobab. If you're on a self-drive, head for the designated campsite on Kubu Island. Travelling over the pans under a full moon will enhance the sense of remoteness, and add a haunting beauty to a night under the cleanest of skies. For avid stargazers, travel during the new moon.

THE MOREMI/SAVUTI/CHOBE SELF-DRIVE The continent's most popular self-drive safari route takes in the south-eastern fringes of the Okavango Delta and two of Africa's finest game parks, Moremi and Chobe. It's the real deal with no frills attached, and for the self-drive devotee it doesn't get much better than this.

A SUNSET CRUISE ON THE CHOBE RIVER The Chobe National Park is world renowned for its prolific elephant population, and a sunset cruise, particularly in the winter months, is a great way to make their acquaintance. Chobe Chilwero offers an exclusive option away from the crush, while the Chobe Safari Lodge is the place to be for those with a tighter budget.

THE REMOTENESS OF THE CENTRAL KALAHARI If you want to escape totally the presence of others and the grind of everyday life, disappear somewhere deep into the Central Kalahari. With population densities amongst the lowest in the world, any one of the four reserves and game parks found in the region can offer you a safari in absolute solitude.

KGALAGADI TRANSFRONTIER PARK Incorporating the former Gemsbok National Park, this vast tract of semi-arid wilderness was Africa's first transfrontier park. It offers visitors an amazing variety of bird and animal life, and, if you're travelling in summer, you'll find that the rains can add a spectacular flush of colour to the otherwise parched landscapes.

MOKOLODI NATURE RESERVE No matter your reason for being in the capital city, if there is only one thing you do, make sure it is to visit this private nature reserve. Situated a mere 10 kilometres beyond the outskirts of Gaborone, it offers a variety of plains game species, great white rhino viewing and the chance to walk with elephants. It also provides country-style accommodation – a pleasant alternative to the big city hotels.

OPPOSITE TOP: Visitors to Mokolodi Nature Reserve near Gaborone can experience the thrill of walking with elephants and spending time with them while they undergo training with their handlers (unfortunately rides on the elephants are not on offer).

OPPOSITE BOTTOM: A highlight at Jack's Camp in the Makgadikgadi Pans is a full morning walk with Bushman guides who will explain the art of tracking, their traditional hunting skills and the medicinal uses of various plants.

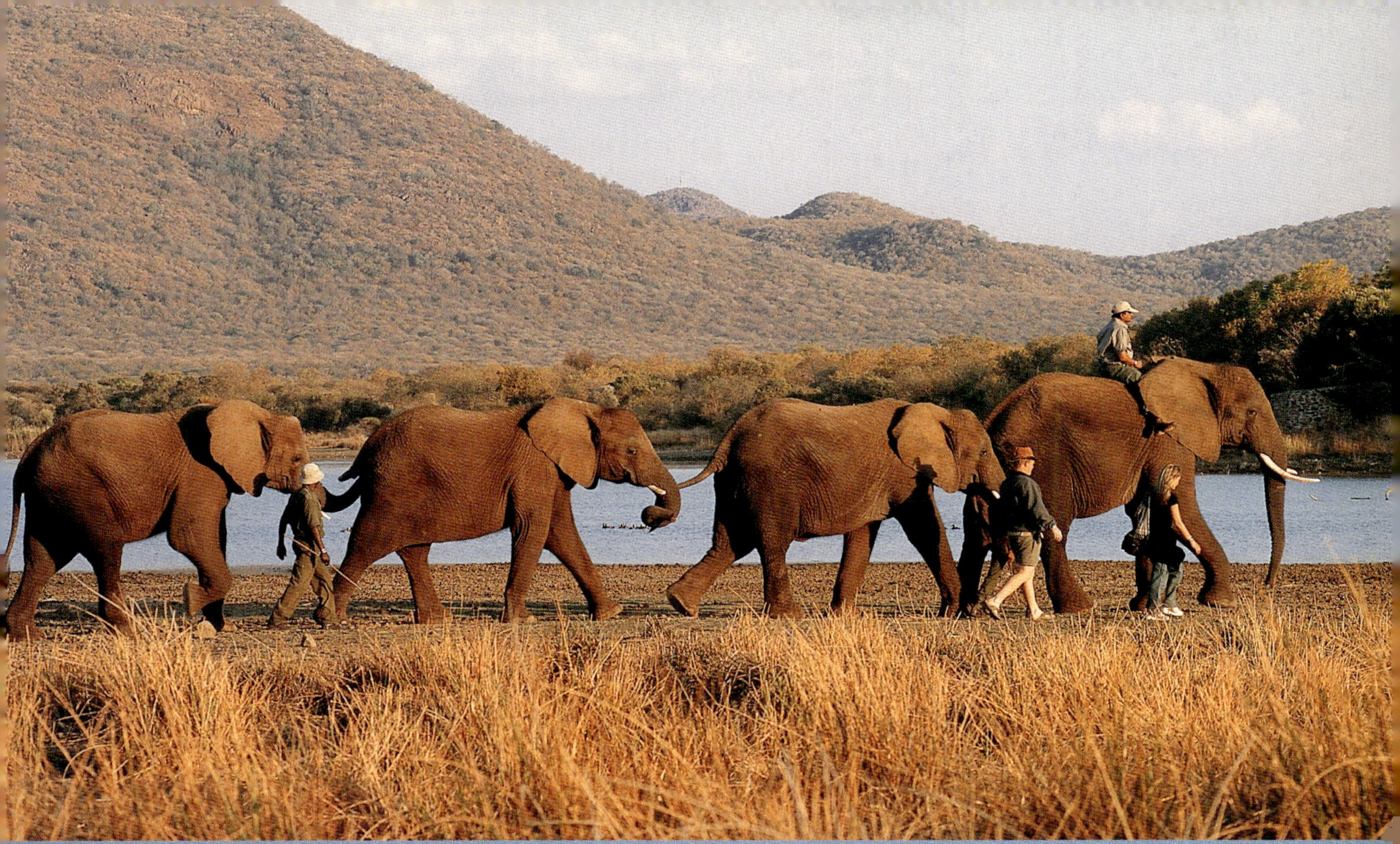

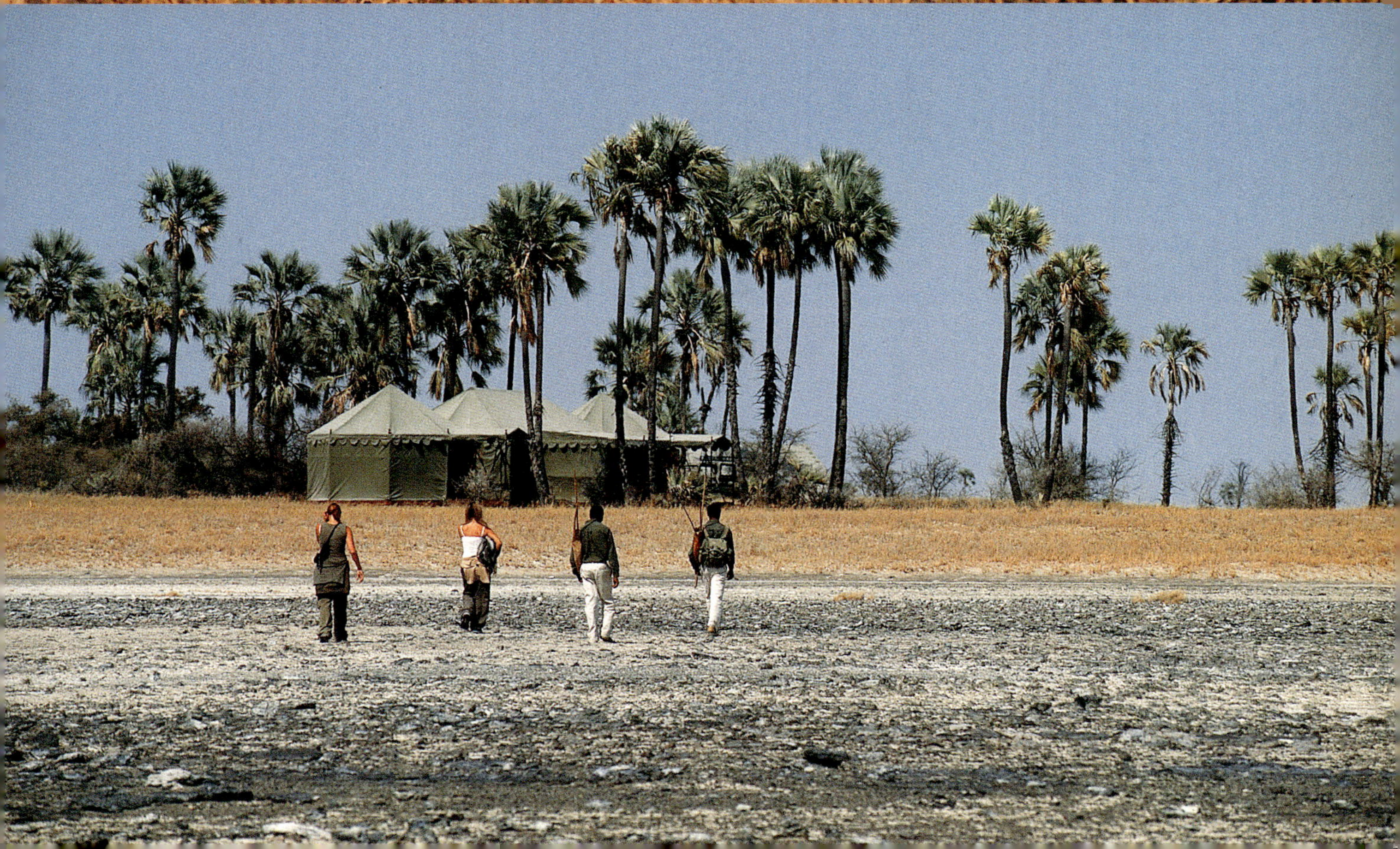

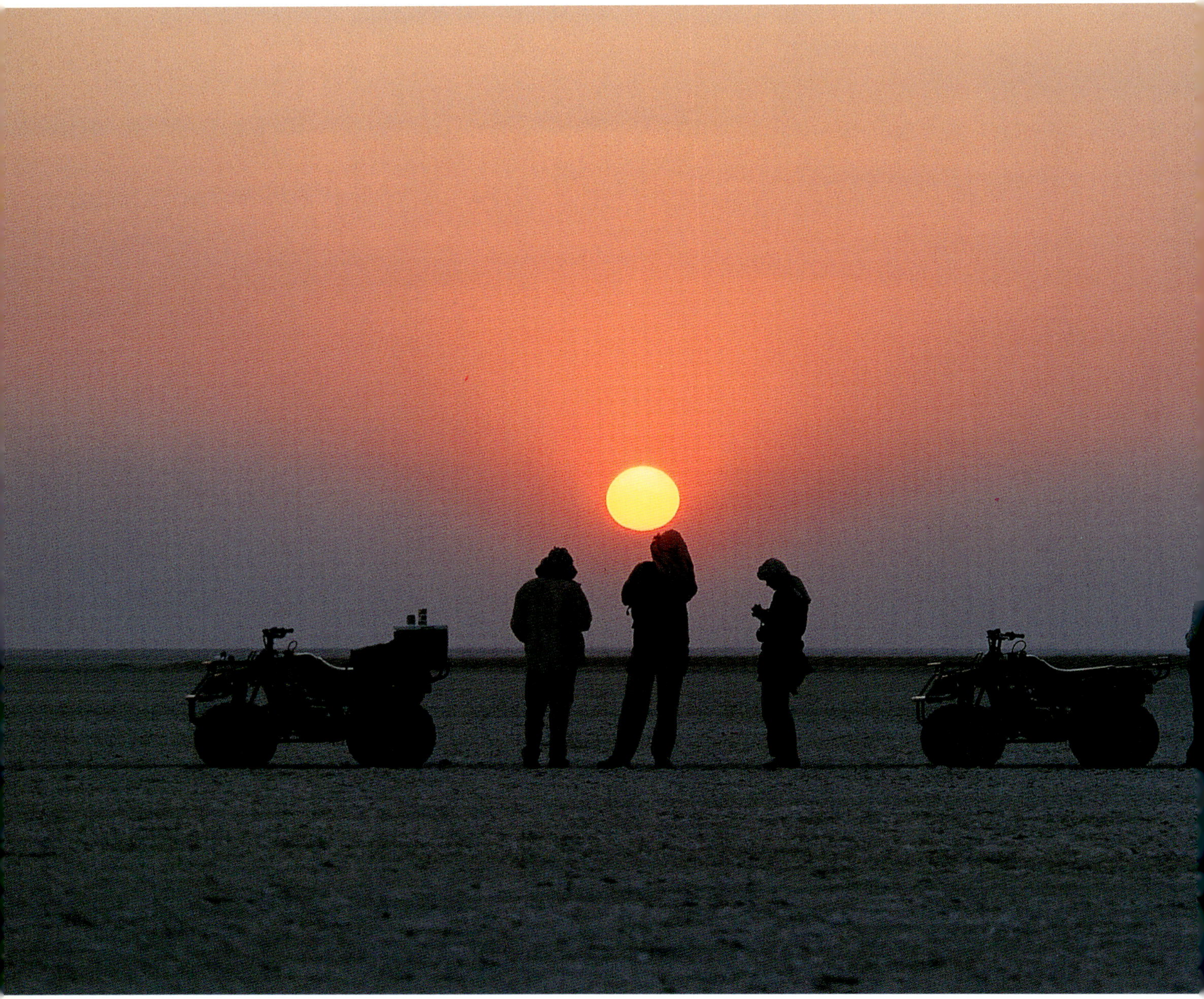

ABOVE LEFT: Quad biking on the Makgadikgadi Pans.
ABOVE RIGHT: Sunset drinks from Livingstone's Baobab
in the Mashatu Game Reserve, Tuli Block.

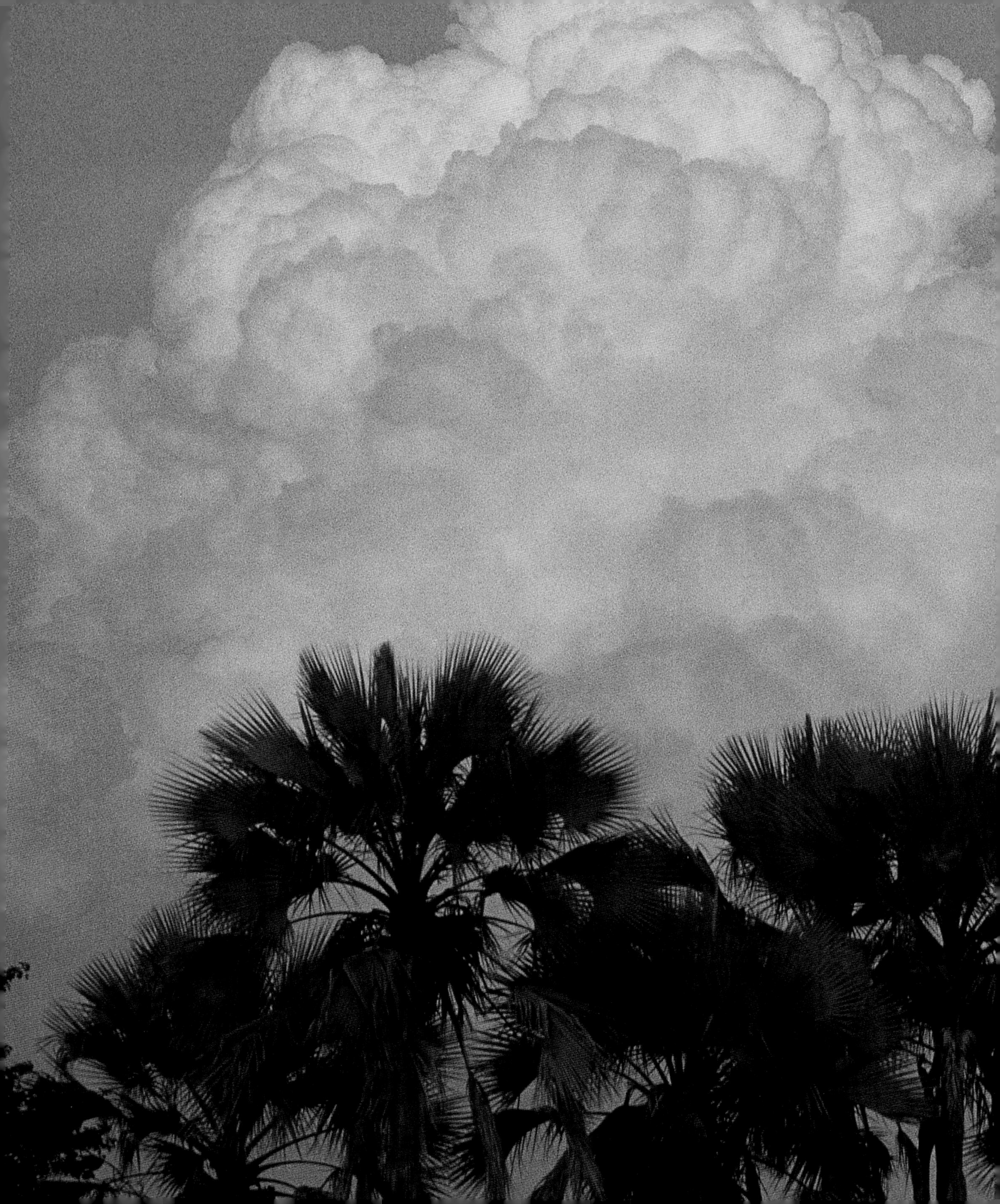

Wherever you may be in Botswana, afternoon thunderstorms are an almost daily occurrence during summer.

Sit back, relax and let the wilderness wash over you as you get poled about the waterways in a *mokoro*.

Spring
Letlhabula (September–October)

The arrival of springtime is confirmed when the migrant bird species begin appearing. Yellow-billed kites and carmine bee-eaters are usually the first to arrive, and woodland kingfishers the last. This will often coincide with the first light rains, sometime in September.

- The **annual catfish runs** are reaching their peak in the Panhandle now, so the tiger fishing is at its best.
- Springtime is music time: The **Kalahari Summer Festival,** an annual charitable music event that celebrates the imminent arrival of summer, is held during September in Gaborone.
- The **hunting season** closes in mid-September.
- Independence Day (Botswana Day) is celebrated on 30 September.
- The **October Beer Festival** is held annually at the Grand Palm Hotel in Gaborone.
- In preparation for the forthcoming rains, the **planting season** is in full swing.
- Throughout the country most of the acacia trees are in bloom, and the baobab, sausage tree and apple leaf are all beginning to flower.
- The arrival of the **heavy rains,** usually by late October, has the pans filling up with water, which allows the elephants to begin their migration away from the Linyanti and Chobe river systems.

BOTSWANA The Insider's Guide

During the summer months the quieter backwaters of the Okavango are filled with colour when the waterlilies, (*Nymphaea nouchal*) come into bloom.

Summer
Selemo (November-Febuary)

With the floodplains sprouting fresh grass cover, the first ungulate calves begin dropping in November, and by mid-December the calving season for wildebeest, impala, tsessebe and warthog is over.

- The water levels are at their lowest in the Panhandle now, heralding the **end of the catfish runs**.
- By early December the rains have soaked the ground, providing perfect conditions for the release of reproductive termites from their natal mounds. Releases may carry on throughout December.
- Towards the end of December, the **first flood waters** of the Okavango River arrive in the far northern regions of the Panhandle.
- Having completed their breeding, the African skimmers will leave the Panhandle region before the new waters begin covering the sandbars on which they nest.
- Thousands of zebra and wildebeest begin their **mini-migrations** in the Makgadikgadi, Linyanti and Savuti regions.
- The sour plum, African mangosteen and marula trees are fruiting in profusion now.

A photographer's dream: autumn sunsets in the Okavango Delta.

Autumn
Dikgakologo (March-April)

Two months or so after first flowing into Botswana, the flood waters reach the upper regions of the Okavango Delta.

- The **last of the heavy rains** are likely to fall during March.
- Maun hosts the official opening of the **photographic** (as opposed to hunting) **tourist season**.
- The **Maitisong Festival,** Botswana's largest arts and dance festival, is held annually in the last week of March or the first week of April in Gaborone.
- Zebra and wildebeest begin their **return migration** towards the regions where water will be available during winter.
- At the start of April, the onset of lower temperatures, the migrant bird species begin leaving for their northern range. By late April, all will have left.
- The **best bream fishing** in the Panhandle begins during April, when the flood waters have settled somewhat.
- Throughout the country the harvest season is coming to an end.
- In mid-April the **hunting season** officially opens.
- With the drying of the pans, the elephants are beginning to head back to the Linyanti and Chobe river systems.

Mopane trees lose their leaves at the tail end of winter. Roan antelope roam the forests seeking out the last of the nutritious leaves, which will be replaced with young shoots once the first rains fall.

Winter
Mariga (May–August)

By mid-winter the flood waters have passed the full length of the Okavango Delta – usually reaching Maun some time towards the end of June.

- The country celebrates its first President on 1 July, **Sir Seretse Khama Day.**
- Wild dogs den during June and July, with their pups due out by early August.
- The **Ghanzi Agricultural Show** is held annually in August.
- The **Desert 1 000**, a popular 4x4 off-road rally that starts from Gaborone and covers 1 000 kilometres across the southern Kalahari, is held annually over winter.
- D'Kar is a small place, and the **Kuru Traditional Dance and Music Festival,** which takes place here in August, is its annual highlight.
- Gaborone plays host to the **Trade Exhibition,** a showcase of the country's trade, industry and agriculture sectors every year during August.

The road between Kanye and Gaborone. Botswana has over 6 500 kilometres of tarred road.

There are not many who travel to Botswana who don't ultimately visit the Okavango Delta. There are five major road routes criss-crossing the country, some with by-roads and side-roads, and others that demand diversions. Whichever you choose, each has its own distinctive appeal and will deliver you to Maun, the 'Gateway to the Okavango'.

en ROUTE
all roads lead to the Okavango

Gabs City

SEE MAP ON PAGE 70

Gaborone, or Gabs City as the locals call it, is one of the world's fastest-growing metropolitan areas. While it only attained city status in 1986, phenomenal growth has seen it turn from a dusty backwater town into one of the continent's most impressive capitals. It has, in the process, become the epitome of a modern African city – embracing the technology, design and fads of the West, but keeping the vibe and pulse of Africa.

With the population now nudging over 300 000 residents, and the boom times set to continue, city planners face the hellish task of trying to control the urban sprawl. Modish high-rise buildings are being constructed throughout the central precinct, 25 000 new residential plots are being added to the city layout and new factories and retail outlets sprout at an unprecedented pace. The rush of development is pushing the suburban limits ever further into the scrubby countryside and, in an attempt to cope with the burgeoning congestion, a network of highways and traffic circles now sweeps Gaborone's outskirts, taking the traffic away from the crowded inner city.

Gabs residents have embraced the material world wholeheartedly, and a bout of healthy consumerism is most definitely helping to fuel the city's growth. The ballooning middle class spends with gusto and the hip set has acquired a swagger that tells of their success and newfound status. Because everyone loves a winner, the city is attracting outside attention. Continental corporations and international agencies are increasingly focusing their expansion plans Gaborone's way, as they look to establish regional offices or representation of some sort in the city.

Gaborone offers visitors almost everything that is expected of a modern, developing city in Africa. It's a comfortable and convenient place to do business, with up-to-date banking and technology services. There's a wide range of accommodation and it's a relatively safe place to be. If you're on holiday time, hang around for at least a few days and let Gabs surprise you.

The Gabs Guide

Eating out

The Bull and Bush – Hearty pub fare, with an expat crowd, and everyone knows where it is.

The Maharaja – The best Indian food in town. Situated right next door to The Bull and Bush.

Primi Piatti – Pizza, pasta and snack-type lunches and dinners, with the hip crowd. Situated in the River Walk.

Mugg & Bean – It's in Game City, and the perfect place to take a breakfast or lunch break while shopping.

Sanitas – Breakfasts and lunches in a tranquil garden setting alongside the Gaborone Dam.

The Blue Tree – Lunch and dinner are served. Situated in the Marupula district.

Mokolodi Restaurant – Elegant dining in the tranquillity of a nature reserve. A short distance outside the city.

Shopping

The River Walk – Pick 'n Pay is the anchor tenant amongst a variety of designer stores and restaurants, and an Exclusive Books. Situated on the road out to the Tlokweng border post.

Game City – Gabs' mega-centre offers everything from major chain outlets and supermarkets to designer stores and restaurants, as well as a Batsalo Books outlet. You can't miss it, just off the Lobatse Road traffic circle.

The Craft Centre – A precinct set in Broadhurst, with a variety of boutiques and arts and craft shops. And the Deli has a great lunch menu.

Kagiso Centre – A complex of non-designer stores and street vendors in Kagiso.

Arts and crafts

Botswanacraft – Situated on the airport side of town, just off the Western Bypass, this large warehouse-type outlet sells all manner of crafts and curios. Tel: +267-392-2487, email: mail@botswanacraft.bw

Thapong Visual Art Centre – A venue with resident painters and sculptors, which hosts ongoing exhibitions and workshops. Tel: +267-316-1771, email: thapong@mega.bw

Thamaga Pottery – Traditional and contemporary pottery and crafts made at Botswelelo Centre, a community-based project on the Kanye road, approximately 40 kilometres outside Gaborone. Tel: +267-399-220, email: botswelelo@gmx.net

A downtown market in the Kagiso District of Gaborone.

Frame Gallery – This gallery, which is situated in the Fairground Centre, usually has a good selection of local art on display.
Gallery Ann – Art and antiques in the Craft Centre complex, Broadhurst. Tel: +267-395-9416.
Botswana National Museum – Houses various permanent exhibitions of historical, cultural and natural history, as well as rotating exhibitions of art and traditional crafts. Tel: +267-397-4616,
website: www.botswana-museum.gov.bw
The Mall – A pedestrian walkway, filled with street vendors selling curios and crafts. Beware the pickpockets.

Nightlife
The Bull and Bush – Bar and live music venue that is an old favourite with the ex-pat crowd.
Chedza Ntemba – Dance the night away with the locals.
Sports Café – Pub meals and bar, with big-screen televisions for the sporty crowd.
The Lizard Lounge – Live and dance music, with a mixed crowd.

Golf
The Phakalane Golf Estate and Hotel Resort – This new estate, situated 10 minutes outside Gaborone on the Francistown road, offers luxury chalets alongside an exceptional golf course. The estate also has superb restaurant and bar facilities, and by December 2004 will have a five-star hotel and health spa, with full conference and convention facilities. Tel: +267-393-0000, email: rayers@phakalane.co.bw
The Gaborone Golf Club – A municipal golf course within the city limits.

Where to stay
The Grand Palm Hotel – Five-star hotel, with casino and grand conference facilities.
Tel: +267-363-7777, email: info@grandpalm.bw
Gaborone Sun – Five stars, with casino.
Tel: +267-392-2777, email: gabhot@info.bw
Cresta Lodge – Middle-of-the-range option.
Tel: +267-397-5375, email: reslodge@cresta.co.bw
Cresta President Hotel – Cheaper option, in the centre of town. Tel: +267-395-3651,
email: respresident@cresta.co.bw

Mokolodi Nature Reserve – Comfortable lodge and a good alternative to the big-city hotel scene.
Tel: +267-596-1955/6, email: mokolodi@info.bw
Hidden Valley – For campers and self-drives this is the only option. Situated in Mokolodi Nature Reserve. Tel: +267-596-1955/6, email: mokolodi@info.bw

Internet café
Every branch of Postnet has internet facilities, and all the major shopping complexes have at least one internet café.

TOP LEFT: Primi Piatti in the River Walk Centre.
TOP RIGHT: Independence Avenue, in the capital Gaborone.
LEFT: The Attorney General's Chambers in the city centre: one of the newest and most impressive high-rise buildings that have recently gone up in Gabs.
ABOVE: Visit any taxi rank or mall parking lot and there is likely to be a game of *morabaraba* on the go.

Gabs–Francistown Route

SEE MAP ON PAGE 69

Back when the Okavango was still a pioneer-type destination, the only way to get to it was the Gabs–Francistown route – that's if you didn't want your vehicle to be completely ruined from attempting to cross the Kalahari. Over the last decade, as the country's roads have been tarred, alternative routes have opened up, making this traditional option a lot less appealing. The road is busy, often congested with commercial trucks and large buses, and, because wayward livestock and pedestrians are always wandering along its verges, it has never been particularly safe to travel.

You'll pass the towns of **Mahalapye** and **Palapaye** in a blink, unless you need fuel, in which case Palapaye is the better option. You can make it to Maun in one day, but, if you don't, the best overnight stops are **Camp Itumela** in Palapye (tel: +267-71-806-771 or 71-509-247) and **Nata Lodge** in Nata (tel: +267-621-1210). Both offer clean and comfortable chalets and camping with self-catering and bar facilities.

To avoid Gaborone, an alternative route is to enter Botswana at the **Martins Drift** border post and head for Francistown via **Selebi Phikwe**. For the late starters leaving Johannesburg, **Kwa Nokeng**, a small lodge and campsite immediately across the border, is a comfortable place for you to spend the night (tel: +267-491-5908).

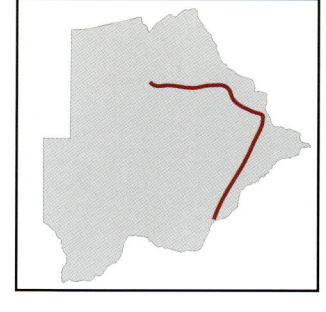

Francistown

With a population of approximately 110 000, Francistown is the country's second largest urban settlement. It is also reputedly the oldest, having been established as a mining community during the 1880s when gold prospecting took place along the banks of the Shashe River. It was Daniel Francis, one of the early mining concessionaires, who gave his name to the town, and ever since then the commercial traditions of Francistown have continued. Today it remains a hub of light industry, textile milling and leather manufacturing.

Palapye, an hour's drive south of Francistown, and Nata, 90 minutes closer to the Okavango, are ideal as overnight stops. You could also spend a night at the **Cresta Thapama Hotel** (tel: +267-241-3872) and **Marang Hotel** (tel:+267-213-991).

Firewood and building timber for sale – a common sight along most of this route.

GROUND BREAKING FOR **BIO-DOM** (PTY) LTD. (CONDOM FACTORY) A FIRST FOR AFRICA

Conserve nature and wildlife

TOP: The Selebi-Phikwe road joins the main Gaborone-Francistown road at Serule.
MIDDLE AND LEFT: Billboards are a common feature along the Gabs-Francistown route.
ABOVE: The main market in Francistown.

The Trans-Kalahari Highway

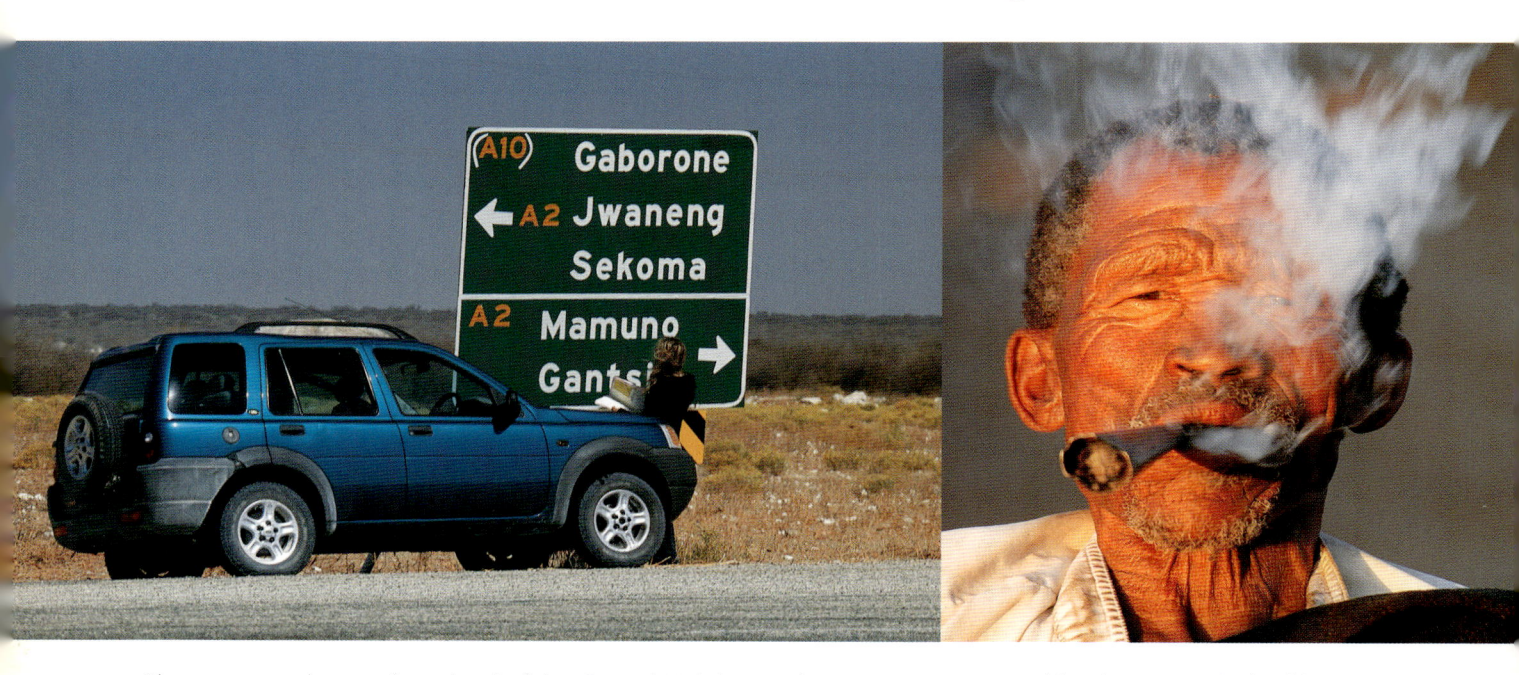

Slicing across the vast hinterland of the Central Kalahari, the Trans-Kalahari Highway offers the most leisurely road route to the Okavango. When entering from the South African side, use the **Pioneer's Gate** border post, avoid the small, nondescript towns of **Lobatse** and **Kanye**, and hit the open road. With long, lonely stretches of tar, this highway takes you on a remote countryside crossing, as it heads west and then north.

Jwaneng, a modern town built solely around a large diamond mine (tours are allowed only with a permit obtained by prior arrangement), and **Kang**, a typical agricultural village, offer the two fuel stops this side of midday. Otherwise it's Ghanzi, another 250 kilometres on.

Ghanzi

Ghanzi is a town that's seeing an upturn in its fortunes. Although the Bushman and Bakgalagadi people were the original inhabitants, the first permanent settlement (a cattle station) was established here back in the 1890s, by the Boer Dorsland Trekkers. They came to this area as it offered the only accessible underground water in the Central Kalahari. Many English-speaking families – mostly cattle ranchers and traders – followed in the early 1900s. After independence, and the downturn in the cattle industry, Ghanzi began to lose prominence, and by the 1990s it had become a forgotten backwater. The revitalisation of the town came with the completion of the Trans-Kalahari Highway and a tar link to Maun, a lifeline that allowed Ghanzi to dust itself off and make a comeback as one of the new frontier towns. The area is now touted as the 'Gateway to the Kalahari', and tourism and the game industry have started to revitalise the local economy. Because it lies close to the Gaborone/Maun/Namibia fork in the Trans-Kalahari Highway, it is a convenient stopover for all three destinations.

Thirty-five kilometres north of Ghanzi is the small village of **D'Kar**, home to various extended family groups of Bushman people. Do take the time to stop here, as one of the best co-operative galleries displaying and selling Bushman art and crafts is situated here. Every year, D'Kar also hosts the **Kuru Traditional Dance and Music Festival** during August. With all aspects of traditional Bushman culture on display, this event is well worth visiting.

Accommodation

Kalahari Arms Hotel – The town's best-known landmark has had a facelift. Comfortable and convenient, it's the best place to stay. Camping and self-catering facilities

are also offered. All tourism activities in the area can be booked from here.
Tel: +267-659-6298, email: afikrainfo@postnet.co.za
Tautona Lodge – A game farm just outside town.
Tel: +267-659-7499, email: tautonalodge@botsnet.bw
D'Kar Hostel and Campsite – Has very basic amenities.
Tel: +267-659-6285

OPPOSITE LEFT: En route along the Trans-Kalahari Highway.
OPPOSITE RIGHT: Ghanzi has the largest urban Bushman community in Botswana.
LEFT: Donkey carts are still commonly used as the primary means of transport in many rural areas.
BELOW: Each year the tiny village of D'Kar hosts the Kuru Traditional Dance and Music Festival.

The Shakawe Route

Anyone arriving from northern Namibia and the Caprivi Strip will enter Botswana at Shakawe, the most northerly settlement on the western side of the country. From this small yet burgeoning riverside village you'll get your first glimpse of the Okavango River. If you're in a hurry you can head straight for **Maun**, almost four hours from here, but if you're on a more leisurely schedule, set aside a good few days to explore the **Panhandle** and **Tsodilo Hills**. Campers and those with a tight budget will find **Drotsky's Cabins** (tel: +267-687-5035, email: drotskys@info.bw), a short distance south of Shakawe and right on the banks of the Okavango, a great base. They offer full or half-day trips on the river. Another 30 kilometres further south, you'll find the tranquillity of **Nxamaseri Lodge** (your accommodation must be booked and no campers are allowed. Tel: +267-687-8015/6, email: nxa.lodge@info.bw) ideal if you want a more exclusive stay away from the bustle of the main road and the busier sections of river. Both places offer fantastic fishing, and Nxamaseri Lodge is one of the very best birding destinations in the Okavango Delta.

Botswana's most memorable rural experiences are to be had on this route. Make it part of your journey and stop off anywhere between Shakawe and the oddly-named **Etsha 6** to bargain for baskets or just observe village life – the people will welcome you warmly. Fuel is available at Shakawe, Etsha 6 and Gumare.

Tsodilo Hills

These three hills form one of Africa's premier Bushman rock art sites and are highly recommended as a stop-off, but make sure you allow a day or two to explore the area. Tsodilo Hills consist of a quartzite outcrop just 40 kilometres west of the main road, standing like a beacon in the otherwise flat surrounding Kalahari sandveld. Archaeological evidence discovered amongst the remains of villages here, including pottery, stone tools and simple jewellery, indicates that various groups used the hills as a trading post, stop-over point and place of abode from as olong ago as 100 000 years. The hills are known to the local !Kung people as the Male, Female and Child, and contain over 4 000 individual paintings, at almost 400 sites, including images of humans, wild and domestic animals, and various geometric patterns and shapes. While some of the paintings may go back a few thousand years, the majority are more recent – dating to the early part of the last millennium. The most modern paintings, of white geometric shapes, are just a few centuries old.

Presently, the only people living beneath the shadows of the three hills are a small extended family of !Kung and a group of Hambukushu, who see Tsodilo as a sacred site, as they believe their people were lowered onto earth by the gods at this site. Besides its cultural heritage, Tsodilo also has immense natural beauty, with the trees, birds and incredible vistas all creating a very special atmosphere.

Tsodilo is now a national monument and Botswana's first World Heritage Site. A small museum complex has been built, and there is also a bush airstrip as well as various designated campsites here. You can also base yourself at one of two lodges in the area (Nxamaseri and Drotsky's Cabins).

For further information, go to:
www.botswana-museum.gov.bw
or national.museum@gov.bw

OPPOSITE: Fishing and birding from boats are the major activities in the Panhandle region.
ABOVE: The Okavango is at its lowest levels in the Panhandle from September to November, and this is when those who live a traditional life along its banks cut grass and reeds for housing material.

The region of the Okavango Delta comprises some
... percent of the total surface of Botswana.

Botswana

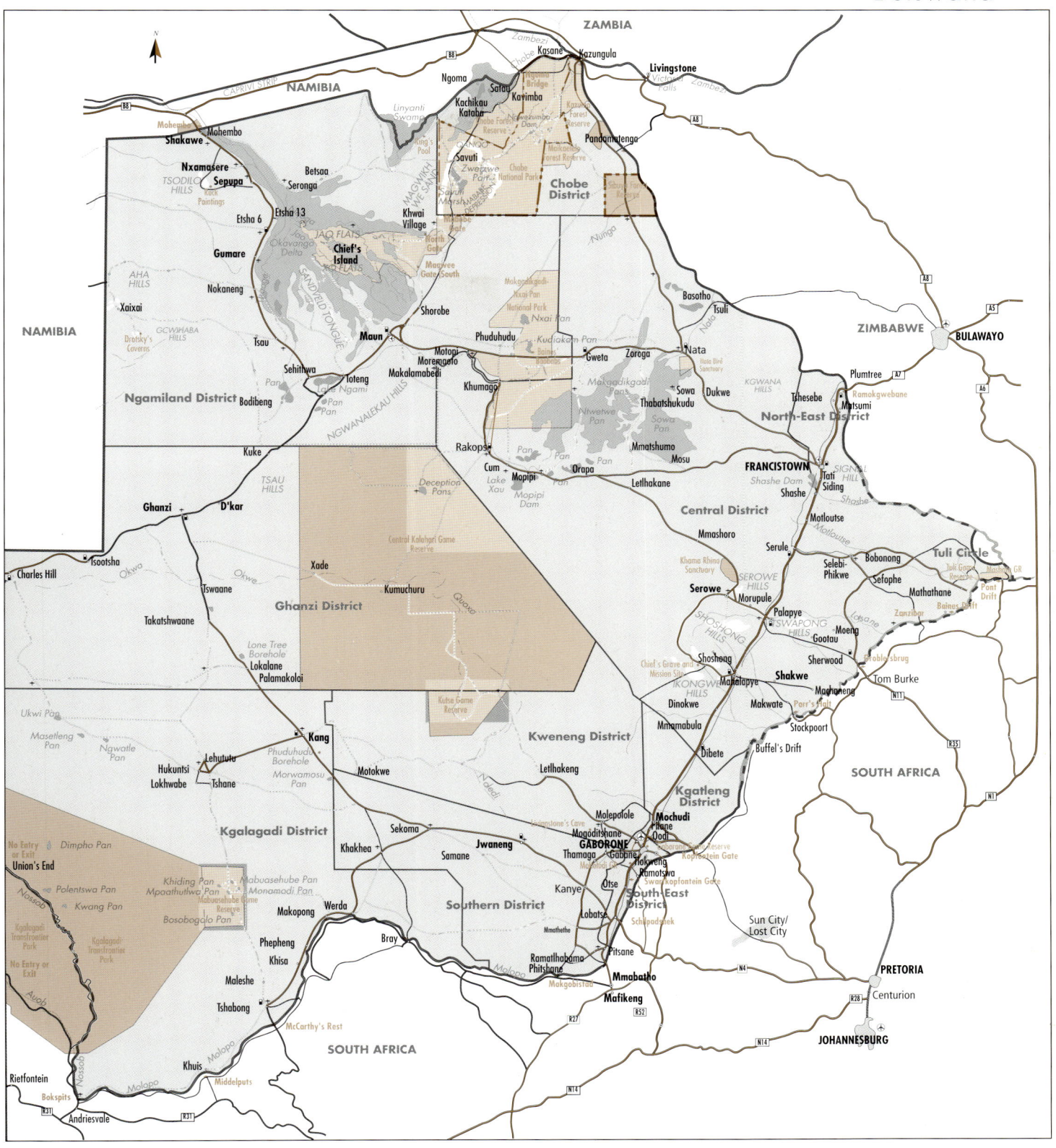

Gaborone

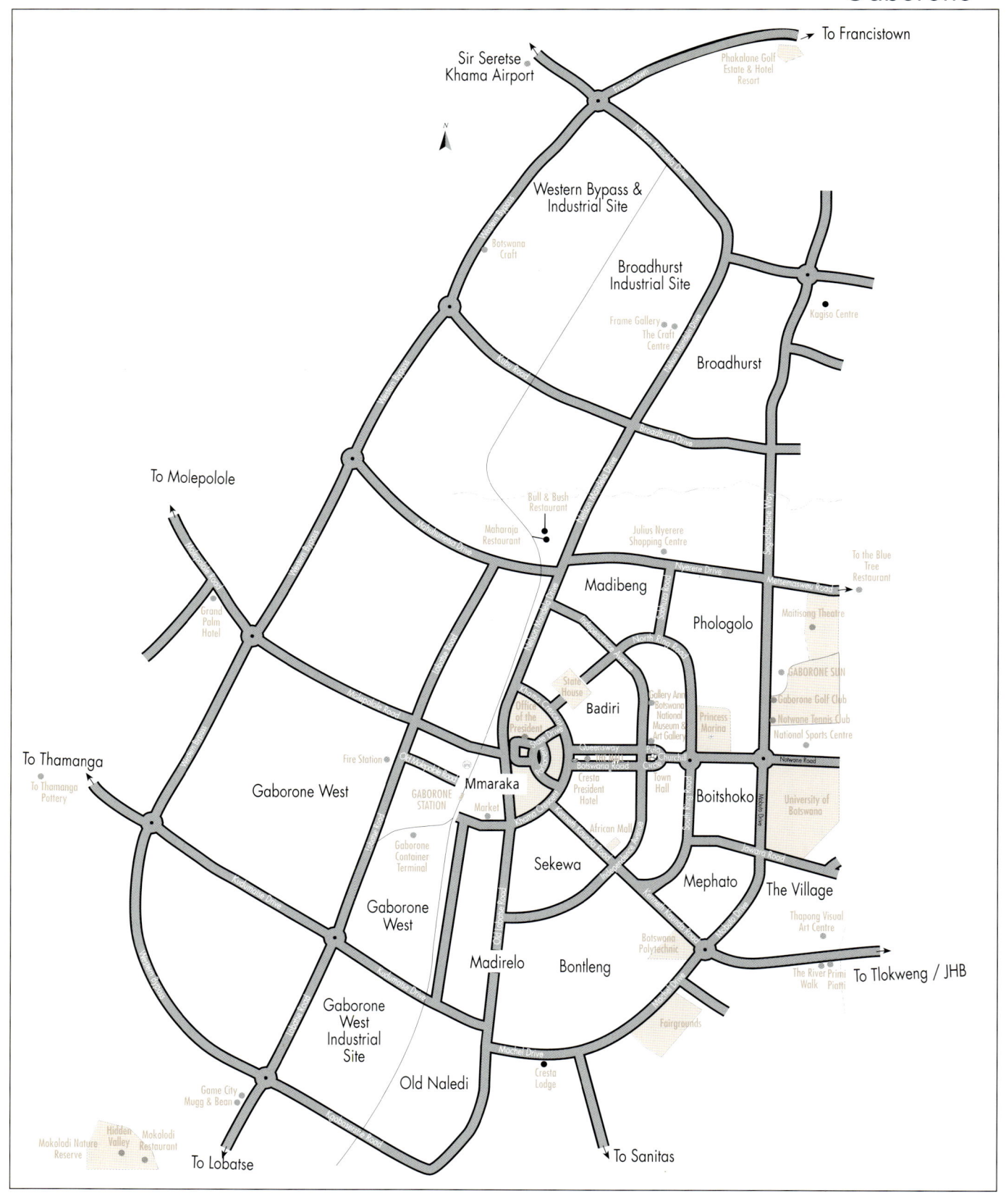

Maun

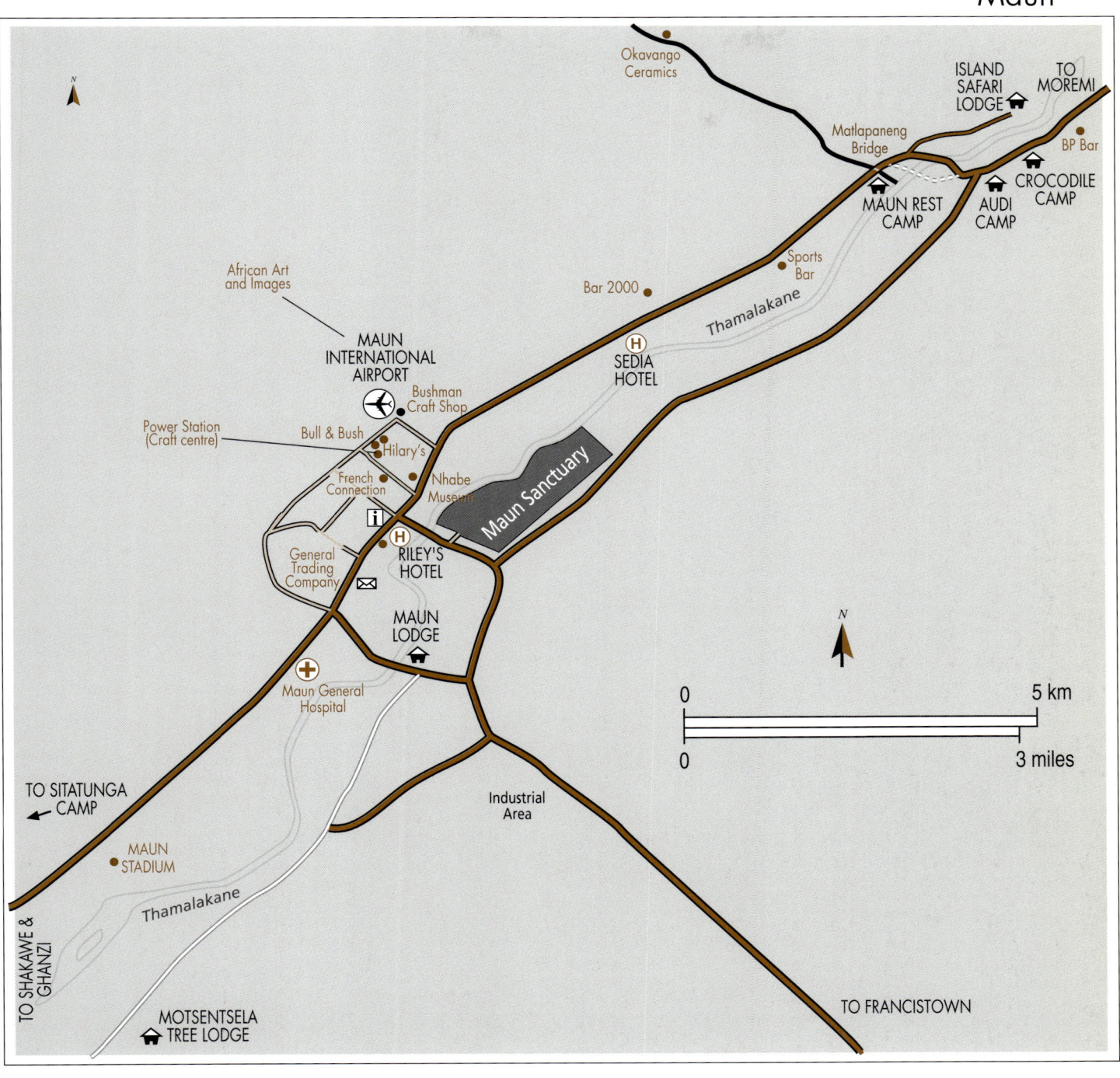

Okavango Delta and Moremi

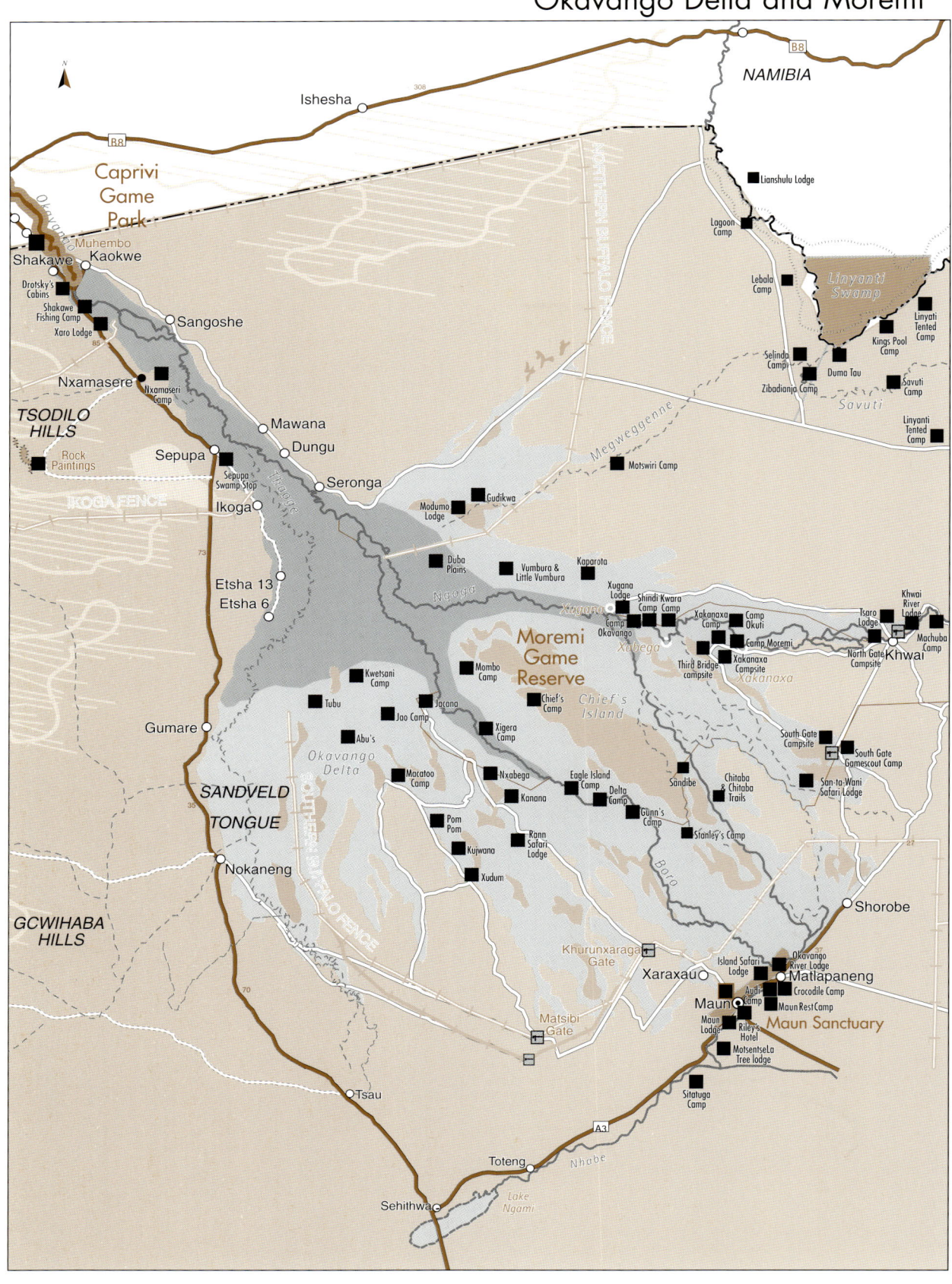

Chobe, Savuti and the Pans

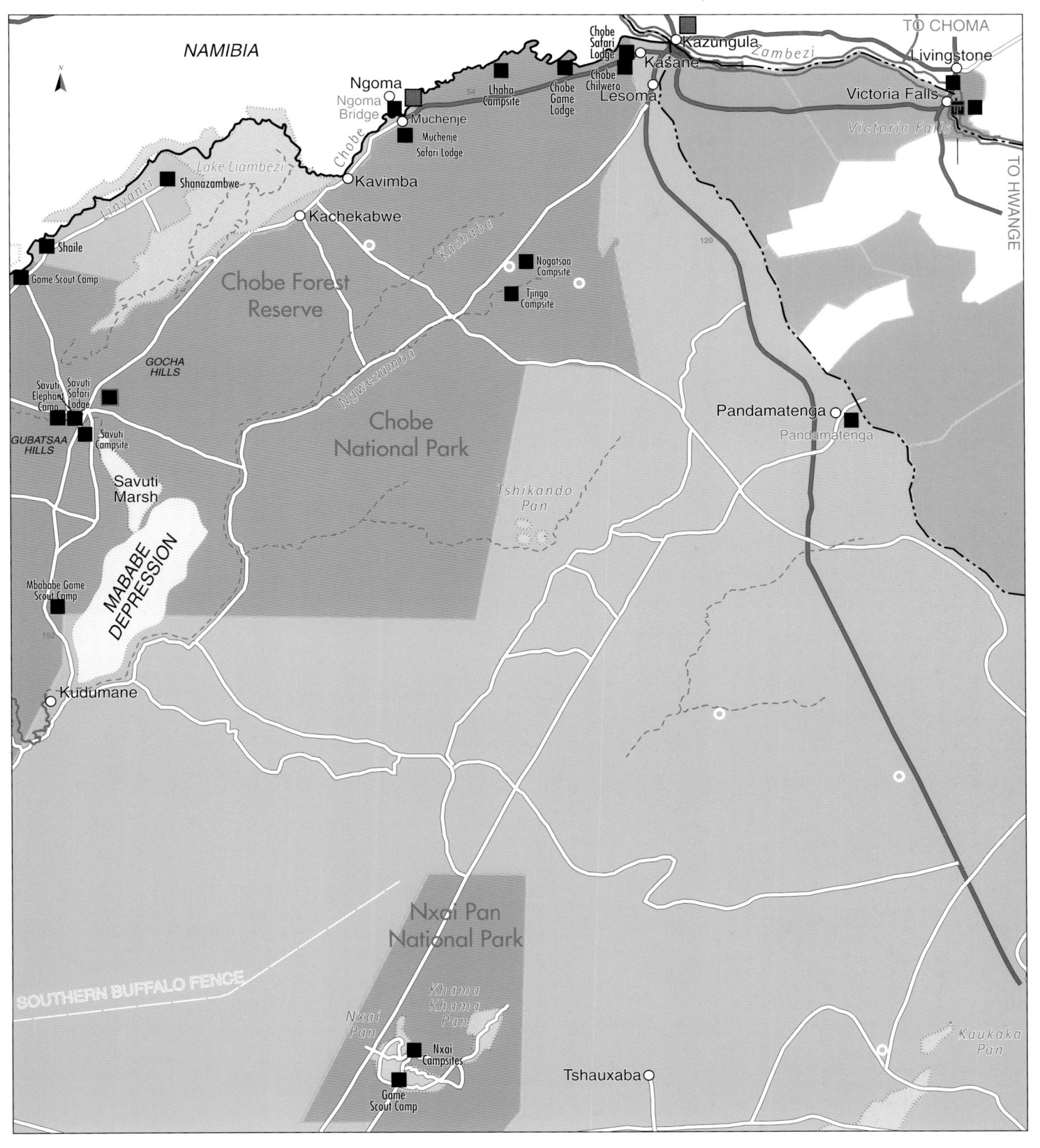

The Tsodilo Hills are known to
and Child, and contain over

TOP: The Van der Post Panel on the Female Hill is the most striking of the rock art sites at Tsodilo Hills.
ABOVE: With its feather-like branches, the wild date palm (*Phoenix reclinata*) dominates the islands along the main river and channels of the Panhandle.

the local !Kung people as the Male, Female (seen here)
4 000 individual paintings at almost 400 different sites.

The Kasane–Nata Route

Kasane itself is not a particularly impressive place, but what falls within the immediate vicinity is. The town acts as the 'Gateway to the Chobe National Park', and as a crossroad for anyone heading to the Victoria Falls from Botswana. As a result it far exceeds Maun as a leading tourist town. Spread out along the banks of the Chobe River, Kasane has a number of hotels, guesthouses and campsites that accommodate all the visitors to the national park.

The town has a decent gallery, **The African Easel Art Gallery**, for you to enjoy during those midday hours outside of game-driving time, as well as a few roadside craft stalls between the town and the **Kazangula ferry**. If you are on your way to Livingstone in Zambia by road, you will have to cross the Chobe River on this ferry. If you are going on the ferry, don't be put off by the queues of trucks: just drive straight to the front. (The possibility of building a bridge across the Chobe River at this site has been mooted, but there are no definite plans as yet.)

Accommodation (Outside the national park)

Chobe Chilwero – This fabulous lodge has the prime spot in a private concession. It boasts stunning views overlooking the Chobe River, and is definitely not for self-drivers or campers. Tel: +267-625-362, email: chilwero@info.bw

Chobe Safari Lodge – This lodge is an old favourite, situated on the banks of the river, and the accommodation closest to the park. There is a large hotel, as well as chalets and a campsite, with a neat sunset deck overlooking the water. Tel: +267-625-0336, email: reservations@chobelodge.co.bw

Mowana Safari Lodge – Large hotel, with nine-hole golf course, on the banks of the Chobe. Tel: +267-625-0300, email: reservations@mowana.cresta.co.bw

Kubu Lodge – This smaller lodge-type accommodation at the quieter end of the river, also offers camping facilities for the more budget-conscious traveller. Tel:+267-625-0312, email: kubu@botsnet.bw

THIS PAGE: With markers such as these, you can't miss the turnoff to Planet Baobab.
OPPOSITE TOP: Nata's Kasane–Maun junction is one of the busiest in Botswana, with an extremely high number of filling stations.
OPPOSITE BOTTOM: Stop off for a round of drinks and a game of pool in a bar and experience the local vibe.

The route south to **Nata** is often referred to as the 'game drive route', as there is always the chance of seeing wildlife of some sort along the way. North of **Pandamatenga**, elephants are common, and buffalo, sable and giraffe can be seen, but less regularly. On the Nata-to-Maun stretch, particularly in the region of the **Makgadikgadi Pans** and **Nxai Pan** turnoffs, ostrich, impala, giraffe and steenbok are common, while elephant and zebra can be seen during the summer months. On both of these sections, keep eyes peeled for the occasional predator early or late in the day.

The village of Nata is another crossroads town, lying at the junction of the roads to Maun and Kasane. It's a grubby place, with more fuel stations than food shops, and an inordinate number of trucks that loiter along the main road. If you're using it as a halfway stop you should avoid the town itself and stay at **Nata Lodge**, about 10 kilometres further along towards Francistown. During the summer months after the first rains, the **Nata Sanctuary** can be a surprisingly rewarding stop for keen birders. This community project is on the northern edge of the pans, and gets flamingo and pelican from time to time, along with another 200 other species that have been recorded here.

Botswana has just under 100 000 telephone lines installed and over 12 000 internet users.

BOTSWANA TELECOMMUNICATIONS CORPORATION

Closing the communication gap

"cheap rate now starts at 6pm!"

PRIMEDIA

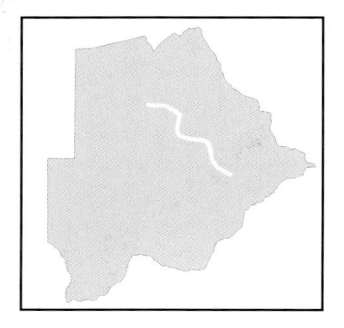

The Royal Route via Serowe

Up until fairly recently this route was very difficult, travelled only by those with sturdy 4x4s and extra time in their itineraries. It has now been tarred right the way through and, because it offers a pleasant alternative to the busier Gabs–Francistown road, it will in all likelihood become the more popular way of reaching the Okavango. The turnoff is at Palapye, and from there it's almost 500 kilometres before this road rejoins the main one, about 150 kilometres from Maun.

There are numerous highlights along the way. **Serowe**, otherwise known as the Royal Village because of its connections with the BaNgwato and the Khama dynasty, is worth a quick stop. Climb **Thathaganyana Hill**, nothing more than an outcrop overlooking the town, to visit the Khama family cemetery, but out of respect first ask permission from the Chief's office at the foot of the hill. This is the resting-place of Sir Seretse Khama, Khama III, Tshekedi and Sechele I. Keen historians, who want to find out the full story of their role in Botswanan history, can visit the Khama III Memorial Museum in town.

The **Khama Rhino Sanctuary** is another 40 kilometres further on and, with a campsite and comfortable chalets, it is the best overnight stop along this route (tel: +267-463-0713, email: krst@botsnet.bw). Started in 1993 as a trust by residents and leaders of the local community, the sanctuary has played a crucial role in the efforts to conserve Botswana's rhino population. Visitors have a great chance of seeing at least one of the 22 white rhino (there is also a single black rhino), as well as a variety of other plains game species, including oryx, red hartebeest, springbok and eland.

Orapa and **Letlhakane**, two unappealing diamond mining towns, follow – but avoid both of them. Next up are the southern reaches of the **Makgadikgadi Pans** and the villages of **Rakops** and **Mopipi**. Maybe it's the isolation, or the first real glimpse of the approaching wilderness, but this section of the trip always has a sense of beautiful desolation about it. The landscapes suddenly look wilder, the villages more ancient and the people more traditional. Resist the urge to race for Maun. Although there are fuel pumps at Rakops and Mopipi, they have been known to be empty on occasion. Serowe and Letlhakane are the more reliable fuel stops. For those who can't make Maun, **Meno A Kwena Tented Camp**, situated along the Boteti River approximately 20 kilometres before the Maun road, is a charming stopover. With the most awesome views from the swimming pool overlooking a water hole on the edge of the Makgadikgadi Pans National Park, guests need merely to venture into its cool waters to watch the procession of zebra drinking below. Maun is just an hour away from here.

LEFT: The United Congregational Church of South Africa is known to the locals as 'London' because it was built by the London Missionary Society back in 1912.
BELOW: The Morupule Colliery Power Station is a landmark on the road between Palapye and Serowe.

The Royal Cemetery, resting place of the Khama dynasty, is atop Thathaganyana Hill in Serowe, reputedly the largest village in southern Africa.

Maun Town

SEE MAP ON PAGE 71

Once the quintessential African frontier town, this gateway to the Okavango has long since outgrown its famed status of yesteryear. Based on a thriving hunting and adventure safari industry that got going in the '60s, the town had three decades of wild times that gave it its regional reputation. But, with those heady days now mere folklore, Maun's residents have to cope with humdrum living in what has become a dull and dusty boomtown.

It was clear that it would head that way once the roads started to be paved and commercial tourism came along. First the Duck Inn closed down, then Woolworths opened its doors and traffic congestion set in – all sure signs that real change was on its way. Confirmation of that came recently with the symbolic ending of two separate eras: Lionel Palmer, the doyen of Maun's hunting heyday and master of some of the town's wildest times, sadly passed away, leaving few of the old school behind; and Alistair Rankin, the embodiment of the '90s photographic safari revolution, left town for greener pastures.

Despite the dust, dirt and donkeys disliked so much by the expats, most of the 30 000-plus citizens of Maun seem to flourish here. For them, Maun is still full of promise, as the wildlife-based tourism industry continues to fuel an economic growth rate averaging over 10 percent. And, with every chance of a career or a job at the very least, why not? Maun will become even bigger, dirtier and more prosperous in the future.

Being the last stop before the Okavango and the national parks, Maun is well supplied and visitors should be able to find most things here. If you do happen to find yourself in town for a night or two, you will be able to keep yourself busy:

▶▶ While the **General Trading Company** in town and the **Bushman Craft Shop** outside the airport offer the best general shopping, don't overlook the ever-growing number of roadside vendors hawking anything from tin trinkets to cane furniture.

▶▶ For art lovers, the **Nhabe Museum** often has a great selection of work by local artists at affordable prices. **African Art and Images**, right outside the airport, has a more pricey collection of art and jewellery, and the **Craft Centre** in the Power Station and **Okavango Ceramics** near Maun offer pottery and general arts and crafts.

▶▶ The **Maun Sanctuary** set along the banks of the Thamalakane River makes for a pleasant late-afternoon stroll away from the bustle of town.

▶▶ To swop safari stories with the ex-pat community, try lunch at the **Power Station** or the **Bull & Bush**.

▶▶ Find the best dinner menus at the **Sports Bar**, **Audi Camp**, **Crocodile Camp** and **Riley's Hotel**.

▶▶ **Hilary's** and the **French Connection** offer healthy and wholesome breakfast and lunch menus.

▶▶ **Riley's Hotel** is perfect for Sunday lunch and a boozy afternoon of live jazz.

▶▶ For the hottest kwaito vibe in town, drink and play pool with the locals at **Bar 2000**, **Mmaleselo Bar** or the **BP Bar**.

Ngunyas, doughnut-like in their form and taste, are everyone's favourite roadside snack.

Anyone who steps outside the Maun Airport terminal will be greeted by this mural that appears on the front of African Art and Images.

Shell
SERVICE SPARES REPAIRS
WIN
ICE BLOCKS
SOLD HERE
TOYOTA

Accommodation

▶▶ **Motsentsela Tree Lodge** – This very affordable up-market safari-style lodge, set in a small game sanctuary 10 kilometres outside of Maun, is the place to stay. A shuttle service is provided, but there's no campsite. Tel: +267-680-0757, email: treelodge@dynabyte.bw

▶▶ **Audi Camp** – Offers tents and a campsite, with an extensive bar and good restaurant. Tel: +267-686-0599, email: audicamp@info.bw

▶▶ **Riley's Hotel** – Middle-of-the-range hotel in the centre of town. Tel: +267-686-0204, email: reservations@rileys.cresta.co.bw

▶▶ **Sedia Hotel** – A little below middle-of-the-range, and a little beyond the centre of town. It also has campsite facilities. Tel: +267-686-0177, email: sedia@info.bw

▶▶ **Crocodile Camp** – Chalets and a campsite, with a bar and restaurant. Tel: +267-686-0796, email: sales@botswana.com

▶▶ **Island Safari Lodge** – Chalets and a campsite, with a bar and restaurant. Tel: +267-686-0300, email: island@info.bw

▶▶ **The Maun Lodge** – Small hotel, with a bar, restaurant and boma eating area. Tel: +267-686-3939, email: maun.lodge@info.bw

▶▶ **Maun Rest Camp** – Clean and spacious campsite close to centre of town. Tel: +267-686-3472, email: simonjoyce@info.bw

OPPOSITE TOP: An aerial view of Maun showing the main commercial district and the new Thamalakane Bridge.
OPPOSITE BOTTOM: Riley's Garage is a landmark in Maun.
BELOW: Donkeys, donkeys and more donkeys: something anyone spending time in Maun cannot fail to notice!

of desert and
DELTA

Whether travelling by air or road, anyone visiting the Okavango Delta cannot but be struck by the stark contrast between the arid landscapes that comprise most of the country en route and the wetland paradise that greets them on arrival. This mix of desert and delta is Botswana's most outstanding physical feature.

Although burning within wildlife management areas is illegal, every year uncontrolled fires throughout the northern regions of Botswana threaten both the environment and the tourism infrastructure.

Most of Botswana experiences low and erratic rainfall. The lowest rainfall, averaging less than 250 millimetres per annum, is recorded in the southern and western regions, and the highest, over 600 millimetres, in the north-east.

The Kalahari – not a true desert

Situated centrally in southern Africa, Botswana also lies within the Kalahari Basin, an internal drainage system formed when the breakup of the super-continent, **Gondwanaland**, occurred over 100 million years ago. With the splitting of the southern continents, Africa experienced uplifting around its edges, which formed the mountain ranges and escarpments of southern and central Africa. Over millions of years these highland regions have endured wind and water erosion that has carried the removed sediment load inwards, to be deposited in the **Kalahari Basin**. This relentless accumulation has created the Kalahari sand mantle: the largest unbroken mass of sand that exists on the planet. Comprising ancient and well-leached soils that are mostly nutrient poor (particularly with regards to their phosphorus and nitrogen levels), the sand mass covers approximately 2.5 million square kilometres. It stretches from northern South Africa, across eastern Namibia and most of Botswana, through eastern Angola and western Zambia and ends up in the Democratic Republic of Congo in central Africa. Although the southern extent – covering South Africa, Namibia and Botswana – is known as the Kalahari Desert, it is in fact not a true desert, but rather an extended region of similar soil and mostly scrub- and acacia-type woodland vegetation, with low and erratic rainfall patterns. In certain areas the Kalahari sands that cover most of Botswana reach depths of over 300 metres.

Three physiographic regions

Beneath the Kalahari's sandy surface lie some of Africa's most ancient rocks. The oldest of these, the 3 500-million-year-old igneous and metamorphic **Basement Complex**, is to be found in the eastern and south-eastern regions of the country. Overlying them is a far younger layer of sedimentary rock, which covers the vast interior region and the north and south. Because Botswana's surface is predominately an eroded one, the country is mostly flat or gently undulating, with an average elevation of just over 1 000 metres. The highest point is the **Otse Hill** in the south-east, which is a mere 1 491 metres above sea level. There are rocky outcrops in the east between Kanye and Francistown, and in the far west, where the Basement Complex reaches the surface.

A typical rural village compound.

The country can be separated into three main physiographic regions:
The wetland region of the Okavango Delta, which comprises approximately three percent of the country.
The Hardveld, where the Basement Complex outcrops in the east and south-east, which comprises approximately 22 percent of the country.
The Sandveld, which consists of thick Kalahari sands and ancient fossil valleys, covering the remaining 75 percent of the country.

At the foot of the Rift Valley

Africa is being torn apart by the **Great African Rift Valley** that extends from the Arabian Peninsula, through the Red Sea and down into East Africa, before it becomes ever shallower as it reaches into southern Africa. This major fault line has had a most dramatic influence on the geology of Botswana. While strictly speaking not a part of the Rift Valley, northern Botswana sits at the very south-western tip, which is sufficiently close to be affected by the ongoing tectonic movement associated with the rifting to the north. Although a tremor registering a magnitude of 6.7 on the Richter Scale was recorded in 1952, the seismic activity is generally not severe enough to be felt, and the depth of the Kalahari sands has an absorbing effect on the shock waves. Nevertheless, the crustal movement has created fault lines within the region that have resulted in the formation of both the Okavango Delta and the Makgadikgadi Pans.

Kalahari–Zimbabwe axis

Approximately seven million years ago the **Okavango River** was linked to the **Limpopo River**, or possibly even the Zambezi River, forming the greatest river system in Africa. That was until a few million years later, when a swath of ground known as the **Kalahari-Zimbabwe axis** was forced up by tectonic activity, separating the two rivers and cutting the Okavango's access to the Indian Ocean. A super-lake covering almost 200 000 square kilometres at its peak soon formed, as the waters of the Okavango became trapped to the west of the higher ground. This lake was also fed by other systems, the **Chobe-Zambezi** and **Kwando-Linyanti** in particular, but, when further crustal activity cut off the water supply from the Okavango River approximately 750 000 years ago, it began to dry up. The result was the formation of the Okavango Delta as it is today, and, once the lake had dried out totally, the Makgadikgadi Pans.

Four drainage sytems

Besides the geological upheavals, the country's drainage patterns have also been affected by variations in the regional climate. Over the last 50 000 years, northern Botswana has undergone a series of alternating climatic cycles that has resulted in four drier periods and five wet ones. Presently in another dry cycle, the country's hydrology now consists of four major drainage systems:

The Okavango River system, which includes the Selinda Spillway, the Thamalakane and Boteti rivers and the Makgadikgadi Pans. This system forms an inland delta with no access to the sea.
The Chobe River system, which includes the Kwando River and Linyanti Marsh. The water from this system in turn flows into the Zambezi River, immediately east of Kasane.
The Limpopo River system, which includes the Shasi and Maklautsi rivers in eastern Botswana.
The Auob-Nossob and Molopo rivers in the far south.

Only two of these systems, the Okavango and Chobe, are perennial, and both have their sources north of Botswana. The flow patterns of the others are totally dependent on local rainfall levels and in dry periods the Auob-Nossob and Molopo system may not flow for years, while the Limpopo River usually dries out by the end of summer. Of all the surface water in Botswana, almost 95 percent is found in the Okavango system.

A reminder that predators are about.

At the southern extremity of the Okavango Delta the last of the flood waters pass through this floodplain channel during August and September, before feeding into the Thamalakane River.

With a steady procession of wildlife coming down to drink during winter, Rock Pan on the Savuti Channel is a great place for photographers to spend time.

on SAFARI

Botswana is a unique safari destination: wild, pristine and expansive. Nowhere else in Africa offers visitors such an alluring diversity of wilderness. Thirty-nine percent of the land is protected in some form, including almost the entire northern third of the country and large parts of the central and southern regions. These wild areas offer visitors unsurpassed opportunities to view a spectacular variety of plant and animal life. The major drawcard has always been the magic and mystery of the Okavango Delta, southern Africa's largest wetland. No less captivating are the smaller river systems of the Linyanti, Kwando and Selinda, along the northern border with Namibia. All these wetlands draw immense concentrations of wildlife during the winter months and a fascinating diversity of birdlife in summer.

Unique and diverse

SEE THE MAPS ON PAGES 72 AND 73

Chobe National Park and **Moremi Game Reserve**, the pride of the country's protected natural heritage, are two of the continent's greatest reserves. While both are dominated by river systems, they also contain a mosaic of grassland and dry woodland that is packed with most game species. For those in search of remoteness, the vast and semi-arid parks and reserves of the **Kalahari** provide a stunning contrast to their northern neighbours. Botswana's portfolio is completed by two most distinctive regions, the startling flatness of the **Makgadikgadi Pans** and the haunting beauty of the rock-strewn **Tuli Block**.

the privacy afforded to guests while they are on safari. Government policy actually limits the numbers of guests allowed at any one time, making the experience that much more exclusive and ultimately memorable. This factor has made Botswana one of the more attractive options when choosing a safari destination. Generally, the most rewarding safari will be one incorporating a combination of areas and lodge types.

LEFT: If you're heading north from Maun, the Moremi Game Reserve is an ideal first stop on your self-drive safari.
ABOVE: Summer thunderstorms produce the most remarkable colours after the rains have passed.

All the national parks and reserves have private concessions (with an average size of about 100 000 hectares) on their outskirts, and those in the Okavango literally ring the Moremi Game Reserve. This system of allocating 15-year leases to private operators has for the most part been successful, as it serves the twin purposes of ensuring the operator conserves the concession while the government is able to control impact levels. Because they also offer night drives and limited off-road driving, some of the finest game viewing is to be experienced in these concessions. Their greatest attraction, though, is

The major national parks and game reserves

1. Chobe National Park – 11 700 square kilometres – Includes the well-known Savuti Marsh.

2. Moremi Game Reserve – 3 800 square kilometres – Covers almost 25 percent of the Okavango Delta.

3. Makgadikgadi Pans and Nxai Pan National Park – 7 300 square kilometres – These parks were integrated in 1993.

4. Central Kalahari Game Reserve – 52 800 square kilometres – One of the largest protected areas in the world.

5. Khutse Game Reserve – 2 590 square kilometres – Lies just south of the Central Kalahari Game Reserve.

6. The Kgalagadi Transfrontier Park – 38 000 square kilometres – Includes the 6 000-square-kilometre Mabuasehube Game Reserve.

The Okavango Delta is one of only two remaining breeding strongholds in southern Africa for the endangered wattled crane.

Wildlife highlights

▶▶ **Africa's largest population of elephants**, well over 100 000 of them and found mostly in the north, roam the country. The best viewing is along the riverfront of the Chobe National Park, the Savuti Marsh and in Savuti Channel region and the private concessions of Kwando, Selinda and Linyanti. Elephants can also be seen throughout the Okavango Delta, but not in the same numbers. Because of the contrasting terrain, the Tuli Block and Nxai Pan are also most definitely worth a visit. The winter months make for better viewing as herds concentrate around water points then.

▶▶ Botswana has the **largest surviving population of wild dog**, Africa's second most endangered carnivore. As there are thought to be no more than between 600 and 1 000 dogs ranging the whole country, sightings of this species are a lot less common than of the other large predators. Best viewing is usually during the winter months when the dogs become sedentary around a chosen den site. While they may be seen within all the protected areas, your best chances of seeing them are the camps in the private concessions of Kwando, Linyanti and Selinda, the Moremi Game Reserve and the private concessions of Vumbura, Chitabe and Sandibi in the Okavango Delta.

▶▶ During the summer months the greater Makgadikgadi Pans and Nxai Pan region plays host to an

Game drives during the peak flood period have an added element of adventure to them. If you do get stuck, your guide should be able to get you out, and, if not, most camps have a standby vehicle that can come to the rescue.

annual zebra and wildebeest migration. While not of the magnitude of the migration that occurs in East Africa, the thousands upon thousands of animals that congregate here are a magnificent spectacle nonetheless. Staying in one of the camps in the Makgadikgadi region or booking with a mobile operator are the best ways to view this parade. November/December and February/March are the peak viewing months.

▶▶ Your chances of glimpsing the **elusive brown hyena** are best in the Makgadikgadi region. This threatened species can also be spotted in any of the national parks in the central and southern regions of the country.

▶▶ **Lion, leopard and cheetah** are always on everyone's wish list. All three occur throughout the year in the protected areas. While you're likely to see lions on most safaris, because of the leopard's habits and cheetah's numbers, these wild cats will be seen less regularly. The best places for leopard are the camps in the Moremi Game Reserve and the Okavango Delta. Cheetahs prefer slightly drier habitats and are found more commonly in the Savuti Marsh and Savuti Channel, as well as on the open floodplain habitats of the Moremi Game Reserve and the Okavango Delta. The Kgalagadi Transfrontier Park also has a healthy cheetah population.

▶▶ **The largest crocodiles**, with some specimens reaching over four metres in length, occur in the Panhandle region. The best months for viewing are August to December when the Okavango River is at its lowest levels.

▶▶ **White rhinoceros** have recently been reintroduced to the Okavango Delta, and Mombo on the northern edge of the Moremi Game Reserve is the best place to see them. It is highly likely, though, that within the next few years they will be seen throughout the Delta.

▶▶ **Sable and roan antelope** are the most sought after of the antelope species. The Vumbura concession in the northern regions of the Okavango Delta, the Kwando, Selinda and Linyanti concessions, and the Chobe National Park offer the best chance for you to make a sighting. **Sitatunga** is another rare antelope and is best seen in the Panhandle and from the water camps of the Okavango Delta when water levels are at their lowest.

▶▶ **A large herd of buffalo** moving across the plains is one of Africa's most impressive sites. Botswana still has large herds of buffalo, with the best sightings along the Chobe riverfront, in the northern regions of the Okavango and on Chief's Island in the Moremi Game Reserve.

▶▶ **Red lechwe**, an antelope species in the reedbuck family, is one of Botswana's most unusual animals. Fortunately, it can be seen almost everywhere within the Okavango and in most places along the water in the Kwando, Linyanti and Selinda concessions.

▶▶ **Great birding** can be enjoyed from September through to early March. The migrants have arrived and the flood levels and weather conditions generally allow for optimum feeding conditions during these months. All the wetland areas are havens for water birds and woodland species, while Kgalagadi Transfrontier Park and Chobe National Park offer fantastic raptor sightings.

▶▶ **African skimmers** are best seen in the Panhandle and along the Chobe and Linyanti river systems from August to December. For **Pel's fishing owl**, head to the Panhandle or any of the water camps in the Okavango Delta throughout the year. **Wattled crane** and **slaty egret** are likely to be seen from most of the camps in the Okavango, and, to view colonies of **carmine bee-eaters**, visit the northern Panhandle and the Chobe and Linyanti systems during the months of September, October and November. The **flamingo flocks** arrive on the Makgadikgadi Pans over the summer months, but their numbers and duration of stay are highly dependent on the water levels.

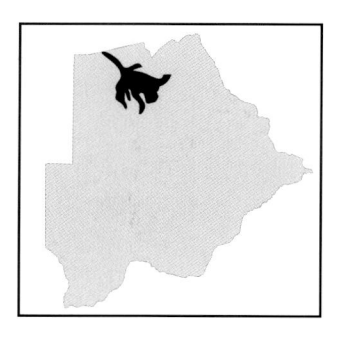

The Okavango Delta & Moremi

SEE MAPS ON PAGES 69 AND 72

A Paradise, The Last Eden, Jewel of the Kalahari, A Wetland Wonder, An Oasis – these are some of the many descriptions used by writers, photographers and filmmakers in an attempt to describe the captivating nature of the Okavango Delta. The truth is that it is all these and so much more, and that's why wildlife enthusiasts of every ilk have always been drawn to this most spectacular of wilderness areas. The Okavango is without doubt one of Africa's top natural wonders, and, for anyone attracted to the outdoors, it simply has to be seen.

Commonly referred to as a delta, and sometimes, less correctly, as a swamp, the Okavango is in fact an inland delta or alluvial fan. Created by faulting associated with regional movements in the continental crust, it is the largest of its type to be found anywhere in the world. The system has its beginnings over 1 200 kilometres away in the **Angolan Highlands**, where it draws its waters from a catchment area covering approximately 150 000 square kilometres. Known as the **Cubango River** (the Quito River is a main tributary), as it flows in a southerly direction through Angola, it becomes the **Kavango River** once it enters Namibia, where it bends eastwards, forming the border between the two countries for a few hundred kilometres. It then sweeps southwards again as it crosses the narrow **Caprivi Strip** before entering Botswana, where it becomes known by its more famous name, the **Okavango River**.

The most outstanding feature of the system is the annual water cycle of local summer rainfall followed by the winter flood waters that permeate throughout the Delta. The paradox of the cycle is that the flood waters are at their highest levels during the dry season and at their lowest during the wet season. It is this crucial year-round availability of water that allows the Delta to support the diversity of life to be found here. The greater region is a semi-arid one, and, without the water and the sediment-load of nutrients that gets brought with it, the existing plant and animal densities would simply not survive.

Delta dynamics

▶▶ The Okavango consists of two distinctive regions. In the north, there is the linear **Panhandle**, extending for approximately 90 kilometres, over the course of which the river flows mostly as a single, meandering body of water flanked by narrow floodplains. To the south, the river then breaks up into a number of channels as it enters the fan-shaped main body of the system, known as **the Delta**.

▶▶ The upper reaches of the Delta consist of **permanent water** held in lagoons and deep water channels, while the middle and lower reaches comprise an extensive network of floodplains and islands, which experience a **seasonal pattern of flooding.**

▶▶ The **Gumare Fault** divides the Panhandle from the main body of the Delta, and the **Thamalakane-Kunyare Fault** that passes through Maun forms the bottom end of the system. The ground between the two fault lines is slightly lower than that on either side of them and so forms a trough-like depression, which serves to slow and eventually trap the water flow. There are also smaller fault lines on either side of the Panhandle, running parallel to the river.

▶▶ The distance between **Mohembo**, at the top, and Maun, at the bottom, is almost 250 kilometres. The height of the ground changes a mere 65 metres over this distance, which contributes to the slowing of the flow, the subsequent process of sheet flooding and of sediment deposition in the characteristic fan shape.

▶▶ Below the Panhandle, the Okavango River splits into three main channel systems:
1. **The Nqoga**, which flows in an easterly direction and becomes the Maunachira. This in turn splits into the Kwhai and the Mboroga, with the latter splitting again into the Santantadibe and Gomoti before they end up as the Thamalakane River near Maun.
2. **The Jao-Boro** system that flows roughly down the centre and joins up with the Thamalakane.
3. **The Thaoge**, which flows along the furthest western edge of the Delta. During years of extremely high flood

levels, water from this channel may push into **Lake Ngami** on the south-western edge of the Okavango.

▶▶ Between 10 000 million and 15 000 million **cubic metres of water** enter the system on an annual basis, with approximately 75 percent originating from the source region and 25 percent from local rainfall.

▶▶ The early **flood waters** reach Mohembo in late December and January, pass through the central regions of the Delta in April and May, before reaching Maun by late June. The highest average levels are found from April through to July, and the lowest from November through to late January.

▶▶ Possibly the most amazing of all the facts is that over **95 percent of the water** gets lost to the atmosphere. This occurs through evaporation directly off open bodies of water, such as lagoons and rivers, and via evapotranspiration, which takes place through plant material. Just three percent will seep into the groundwater reserves and only two percent flows into the Thamalakane River.

▶▶ The Okavango is a dynamic system with each flood cycle being different from the last. On a seasonal basis, both **local and regional rainfall levels** will affect the annual water cycle, as will the process of channel development and channel switching. Hippopotamus activity, which keeps the water channels open, also plays a role. Unfortunately, human activity, in the form of tourism, is highly likely to become a major factor in the future.

▶▶ The main **directional flows** and the volumes of water carried change on a medium- to long-term basis. While in past years most of the water flowed down the Thaoge, presently it carries only about 16 percent of the water. The Nqoga carries just over 60 percent and the balance flows via the Jao-Boro system. Recent monitoring of these channels indicates that the Nqoga system may be beginning to fail and that the Jao-Boro system may be the main course for future floods. The channel switching is responsible for the creation of larger islands and the formation of oxbow lakes and lagoons.

The flood waters will literally arrive overnight, first as a narrow tongue of water, followed by the main flood that can fill a vast floodplain within 24 hours.

▶▶ The river carries in excess of 600 000 tons of **sediment**, mostly in a dissolved form, into the Okavango on an annual basis. Most gets deposited in the Panhandle and the upper reaches of the Delta.

▶▶ The **keystone plant species** of the Okavango is papyrus (*Cypherus papyrus*). This plant dominates the banks of the Panhandle and the channel edges along the upper reaches of the Delta. Growing in dense stands, the papyrus is responsible for the build-up of peat beds, which act as a filtering mechanism for large amounts of nutrients found in the water, and are a primary cause of shifting water flows, because their growth pattern results in bank overflow and the formation of channel blockages.

▶▶ During years of exceptionally high flood levels, a certain amount of outflow will occur via the **Selinda Spillway** in the north-east.

▶▶ One of unique features of the entire Okavango River system is that it is comparatively **pollution free**,

A Paradise, The Last Eden, Jewel of the Kalahari, A Wetland Wonder, An Oasis – these are some of the many descriptions used by writers, photographers and filmmakers in an attempt to describe the captivating beauty of the Okavango Delta.

because no industrial developments, major human settlements, or agricultural activity occur on its banks.

▶▶ The **highest flood level** ever recorded in Maun was in 1955, and the lowest between the years 1993 and 1997.

The Moremi Game Reserve

The Moremi has a proud history, one that in many ways became the precedent for Botswana's successful conservation and tourism policies. Because of indiscriminate hunting, and in the interests of what had been their traditional hunting grounds over the past few hundred years, the local **Batawana** people voluntarily proclaimed the reserve in 1963, in honour of their late leader **Moremi III**. It was officially proclaimed in 1968, enlarged in 1970, with the addition of **Chief's Island**, and then again in the 1990s, when land extending into the Xo Flats and along the northern periphery of Chief's Island was also added. Today, it covers almost 5 000 square kilometres and protects roughly 30 percent of the Okavango Delta.

There are a number of ways to access this haven: book into one of the many camps and lodges found in or right alongside the reserve; join a *mokoro* trip and explore from the waterways and on island walks; or do the overland circuit around the **Mopane Tongue** that fringes the wetlands and takes in **South Gate**, **Third Bridge** and **North Gate**. Whichever you choose, the wildlife is prolific, the waterways enchanting and the experience magical.

The morning coffee break is an established and much enjoyed part of any game drive.

The Chobe River offers some of the most spectacular elephant viewing to be experienced anywhere in Africa.

Chobe National Park

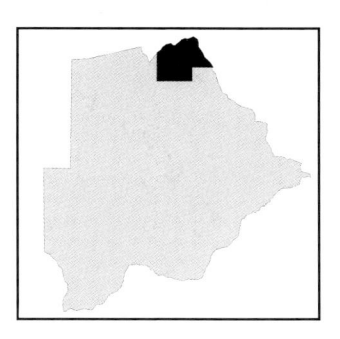

SEE MAPS ON PAGES 69 AND 73

The Okavango may be the country's prize wilderness treasure, but Chobe is the premier national park. It was the first one declared after independence and, like Moremi, came into being in an effort to halt looming environmental destruction. Exploitation by loggers and hunters had begun to take its toll and, in order to curb these activities, it was proclaimed in 1961 and became a full park in 1968. At 11 700 square kilometres, it is the country's third-largest protected area, and for many the most diverse in terms of terrain and species. It is also the most commercial, it must be said, with the Chobe River itself and the spectacular elephant-viewing experienced throughout winter (from May to October) the major attractions. Other highlights while on the riverfront include puku and Chobe bushbuck, two localised antelope species found nowhere else in the region. Large herds of buffalo, often with lions in pursuit, move back and forth between the mainland and the islands, and hippo are to be found on almost every river bend and sandbar.

The **Savuti region** follows closely in popularity, with the sightings at **Pump Pan** having achieved legendary status in the self-drive and mobile markets. Savuti became very well known with the drying of the **Savuti Channel** in 1981 and, although the dry cycle currently persists, the game viewing can still be awesome. The pans and pumped water holes become the main attractions during the dry winters, while in summer most of the action moves to the fertile **Savuti Marsh**. Large herds of zebra and wildebeest, amongst many other species, congregate to graze on the sweeter grasses brought on by the rains.

But don't concentrate on these two localities only, as the less-travelled eastern regions around the **Nogatsaa Pan** and **Tchinga Pan** campsites offer an appealing mix of dry and mopane woodland, and in the far west along the **Linyanti River** there is a secluded stretch of wetland. The general game is not nearly as prolific here, but both these regions provide the chance of sable and roan antelope sightings, and an opportunity to avoid the crush.

Quad bike trails on the Makgadikgadi Pans are conducted with environmental concerns in mind. Riders stick to a single preset route with no off-road driving allowed.

The Makgadikgadi Pans

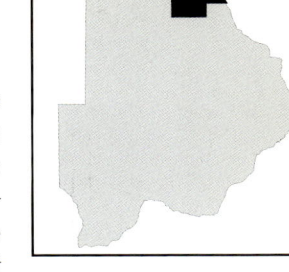

SEE MAP ON PAGE 69

Covering almost 12 000 square kilometres in the central region of the country, two major salt pans, the 6500-square-kilometre Ntwetwe Pan and the slightly smaller Sua Pan comprise the Makgadikgadi Pans complex, the largest on the planet.

They are remnants of an ancient super-lake created approximately seven million years ago after tectonic movement shifted a segment of ground to the south and east of the region. Known as the **Kalahari–Zimbabwe Axis**, this newly elevated region cut the **Okavango River** off from feeding into the **Limpopo River** system and its access to the sea. The resulting lake, at least 60 000 square kilometres in extent and possibly as much as 200 000 square kilometres during wet cycles, began draining with the changing climate patterns of Africa. Its fate was sealed approximately 750 000 years ago, when tectonic activity cut the water supply from the Okavango River. Somewhere between 1 000 and 2 000 years ago, and a number of wet-and-dry cycles later, the lake eventually dried out completely, leaving vast deposits of silicified lake sediment.

The **greater Makgadikgadi system** exists as a single ecological unit covering just over 39 000 square kilometres, which includes the saltpans themselves as well as both the **Makgadikgadi Pans National Park** and **Nxai Pan National Park**. Don't be fooled by the parched landscapes that pervade these areas for most of the year: as soon as the first smattering of rain falls: the region plays host to a fascinating parade of animal life. The water spurs one of Africa's great migrations. Over 25 000 zebra and almost 10 000 blue wildebeest trek here from the **Boteti River** in the west, and they are joined by lesser numbers of animals arriving from the **Linyanti** and **Savuti** regions to the north, all in search of grazing. The animals disperse sometime in March and April once the rainwater pans have dried.

Found in the drier central and southern regions of Botswana, the suricate, one of the smaller members of the mongoose family, is much loved for its highly social and inquisitive nature.

A walk out onto the Pans, with clear 360-degree views, always stirs a sense of awe at the utter starkness of the environment.

The birdlife can also be prolific in wet years. Brine shrimps and algae stir in the salty waters, providing food for thousands of both lesser and greater **flamingoes** that arrive to breed on the southern edges of **Sua Pan**. Pelicans, waders and waterfowl congregate mostly towards the northern edge, where the **Nata River** enters.

While not as obviously impressive, the wildlife to be seen over the rest of the year is just as appealing. Brown hyena and aardvark, two of the most elusive of the nocturnal creatures, are seen regularly, and oryx, caracal, eland, suricate and red hartebeest are other prominent species that act as drawcards for the region. Sightings of elephant, lion, cheetah and kudu are not uncommon in both national parks, and springbok can at times be seen in their thousands on Nxai Pan.

The unmistakable rocky terrain of the Tuli Block.

The Tuli Block

SEE MAP ON PAGE 69

And now for something completely different... the **Tuli Block.** Unlike any other wilderness region in the country, Tuli has its own striking majesty – from the boulder-strewn koppies to craggy mini-mountain tops. Nestled between the **Shashe** and **Limpopo** rivers, this tract of freehold land (a rarity in Botswana as only six percent of the land falls under private ownership) forms a triangle where the international borders of Botswana, Zimbabwe and South Africa meet. Its rugged landscapes, carved from ancient granite and basalt rocks by numerous river systems over millions of years, conjure up images of the old American southwest. Throw in the area's fascinating history and a list of safari options high on adrenalin, and you have possibly the most distinctive corner of the country.

The region's human history dates back to the Stone Age and the subsequent Iron Age, with the **Moutlotse Ruins**, a relic of the great Mwena Mutapa Empire, offering a stunning example. More recent history goes back to the days of Cecil John Rhodes. Chief Moremi III ceded the land to him and his British South Africa Company (BSAC) as part of the deal that guaranteed British protection to what was then Bechuanaland. Rhodes wanted to build a railway line, but found the rocky terrain unsuitable, so gave up the land to private ownership and moved his operations further west. After some of the early battles in the second Anglo-Boer War of 1899–1902 were fought in the region, much of the land was used for agriculture. This was mostly unsuccessful, and tourism has since become the dominant activity.

The safari options here are mostly for the adventurous type, and will particularly suit you if you enjoy plenty of exercise. **Mashatu Game Reserve**, a 30 000-hectare privately-owned wildlife sanctuary, offers a variety of activities from three different camps spread out across the region. Take a ride on the wild side with **Steve Rufus** and one of his 40 horses down on the banks of the Limpopo River. Ride amongst elephant, gallop with zebra and wildebeest, or just cruise the dry riverbeds under the gaze of the towering mashatu trees. If being on the back of a horse is not for you, try a bicycle. Cycling safaris are offered from both **Mashatu Main** and **Mashatu Tented** camps, and, yes, the idea is to go out and find the big game! But don't worry if you're one of the faint-hearted: an armed guide and a backup vehicle accompany the ride. Conventional 4x4 safaris and walking trails are also on offer.

The fact that Mashatu is easily accessible by car, and is only about five hours from Johannesburg, South Africa, is an added attraction. The quickest way to Mashatu is to head for the **Pont Drift** border post, or travel via **Selebi Phikwe** and **Bobonong**. For those with a particularly keen interest in geology and Bushman rock art, the **Lepokole Hills** in the vicinity of Bobonong are worth a visit.

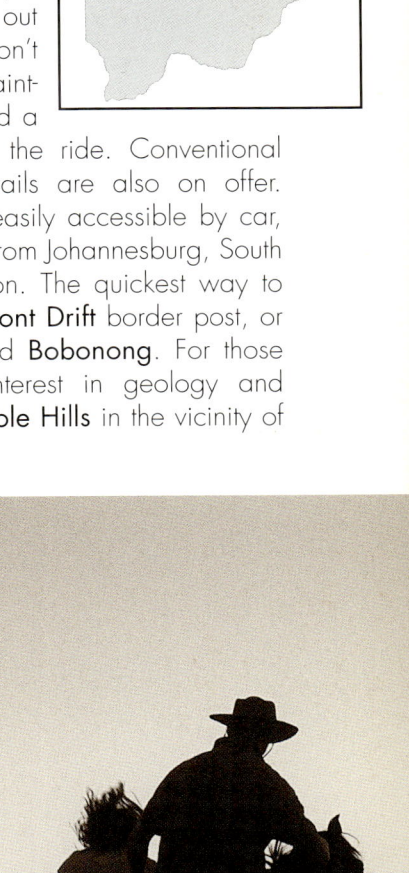

Take a ride on the wild side with Steve Rufus down on the banks of the Limpopo River.

BOTSWANA The Insider's Guide

Surrounded by water year-round, many camps in the Okavango are linked to their game drive routes and airstrips by wooden bridges such as this one at Jao Camp.

Lodge to lodge

With over 150 lodges and camps serving the safari industry, there is likely to be a bed somewhere in the country to suit your liking and budget. The range covers everything from **rustic tented accommodation**, with basic, yet comfortable, facilities, to **sumptuous upmarket camps** that offer the very best in safari style and elegance. Because of the 'high cost–low volume' policy, most options within the protected wildlife areas and the private concessions are of the more stylish variety, catering to those with plenty to spend. If you're on a tight budget, you can book certain community areas (Santawani, for example) and lodges (such as Modumo Lodge) outside the reserves and private concessions, and you can also check for any special out-of-season offers from the major operators. Because the Okavango consists mostly of private concessions and the wetland terrain makes for tricky driving, other than in parts of Moremi, access in private vehicles is not possible. To get around you have to go on what is referred to within the industry as a 'lodge to lodge' or a 'fly-in' safari – moving from one lodge to another lodge using small charter aircraft. Lodges in areas outside of the Okavango are included in a full itinerary. So popular have some of the lodges become that many visitors now choose their ultimate Okavango destination based on a favourite lodge.

The view from the main deck at Little Mombo, which is situated on the very northern tip of Chief's Island.

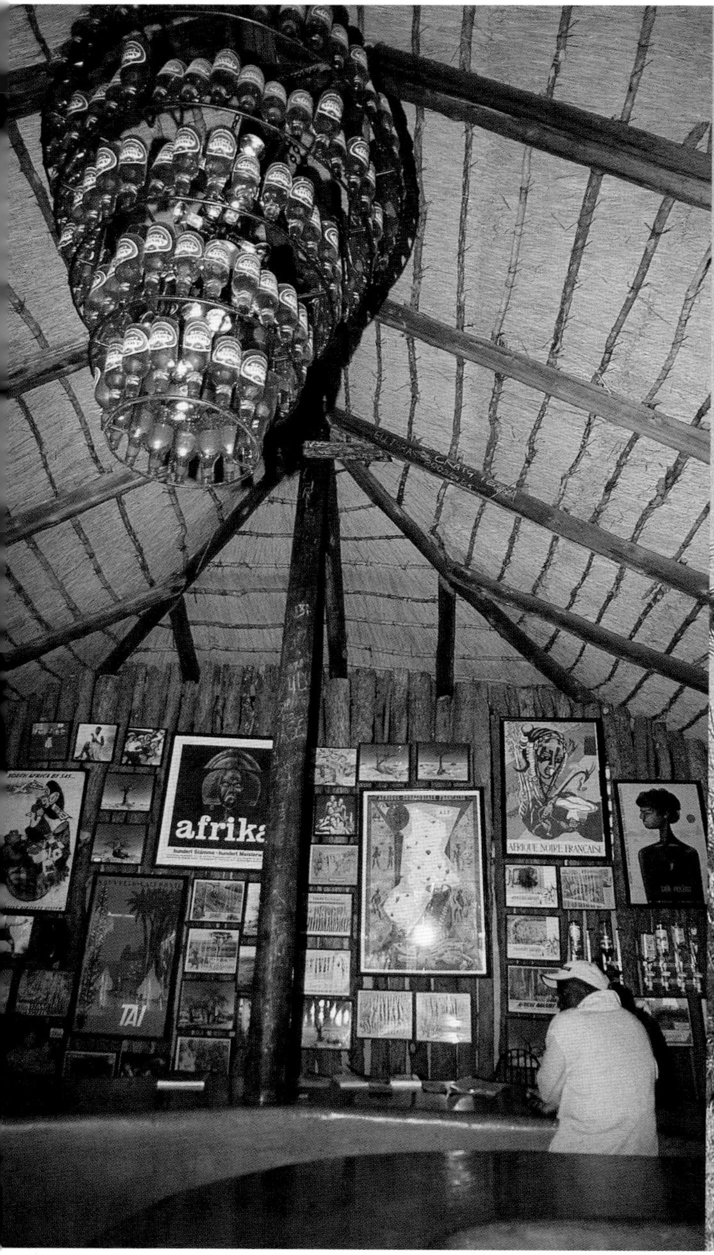
afrika
AFRIQUE NOIRE FRANÇAISE
TAI

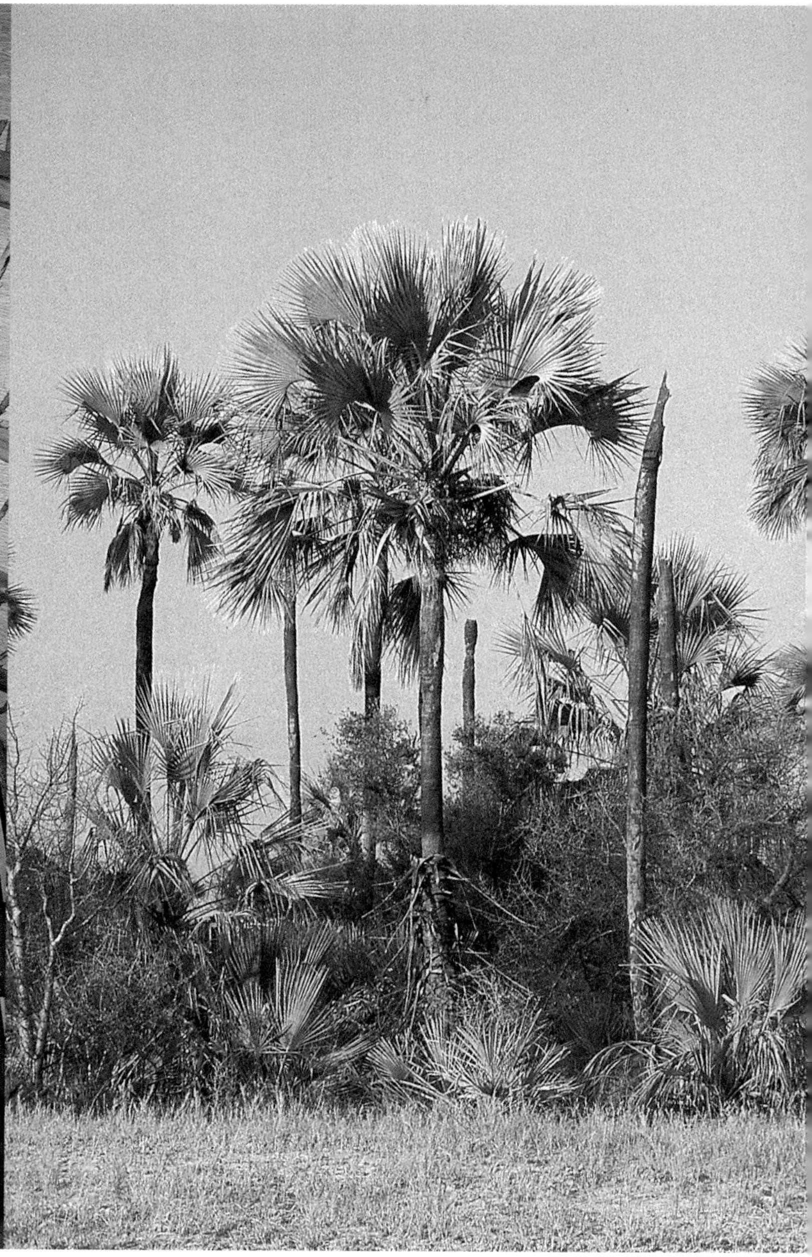

OPPOSITE LEFT: The bar at Planet Baobab in the Makgadikgadi Pans.
MIDDLE: Accommodation tents at Jack's Camp, Makgadikgadi Pans.
ABOVE: Wherever you are staying, if choose to miss the game drive,
cocktail hour on the camp deck is the next best thing.

ABOVE: Savuti Safari Lodge, owned and managed by Desert and Delta Safaris, has three water holes in front of the lodge that attract elephants and other game throughout the year.
OPPOSITE: Safari elegance: dinner under the stars at Chobe Chilwero.

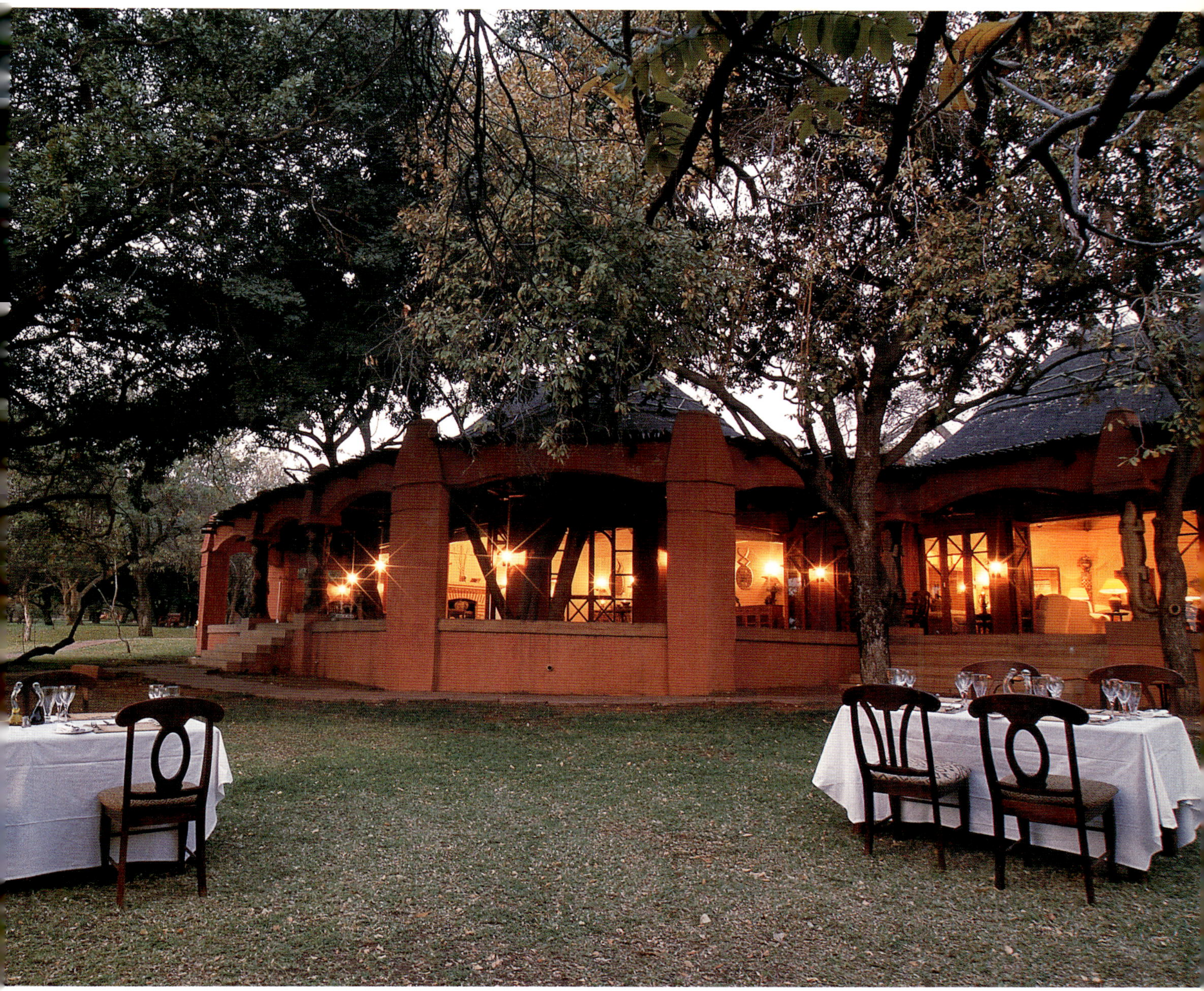

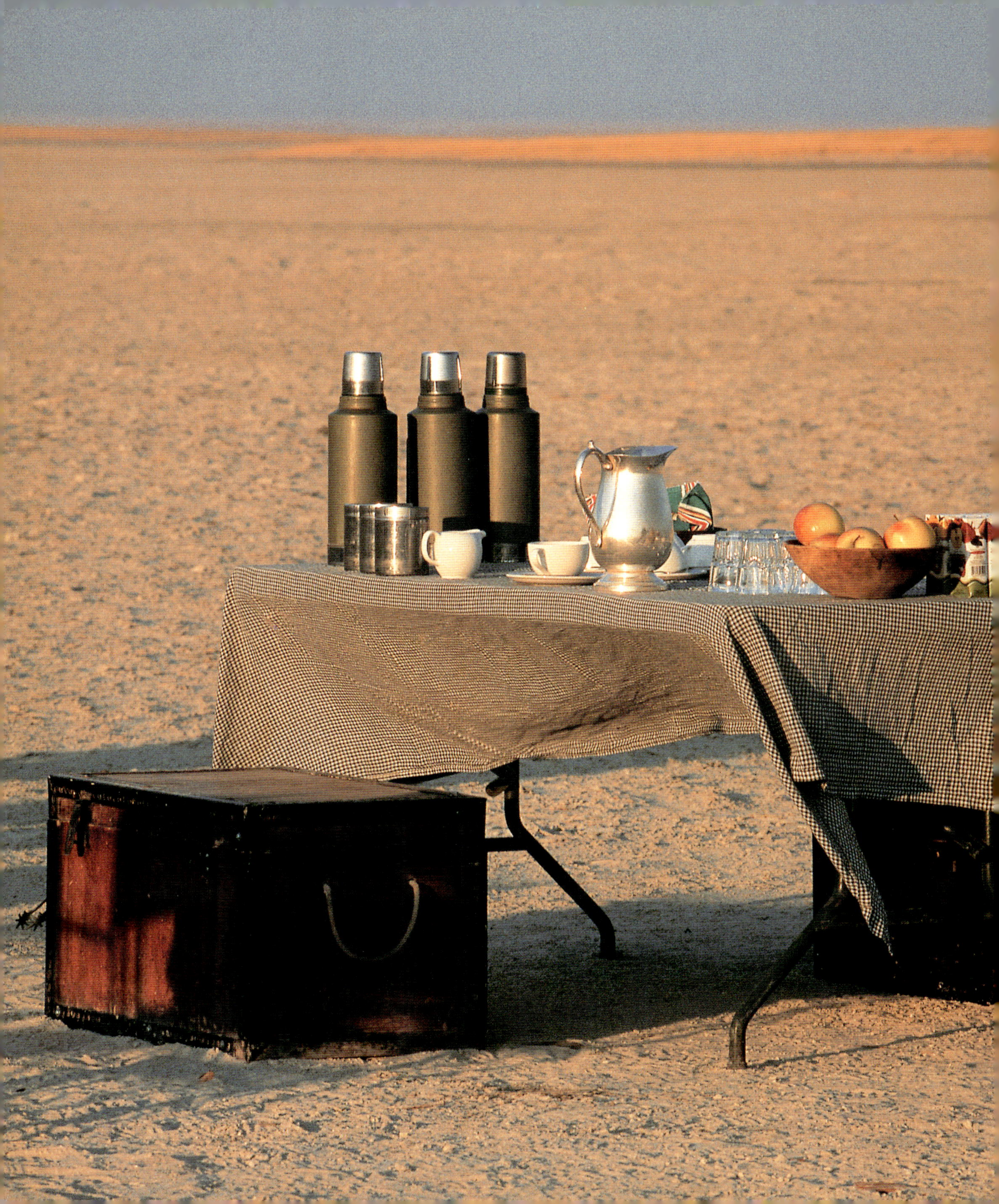

LEFT: Early morning breakfast on the Makgadikgadi Pans.
TOP: The superb views from the King's Pool lounge.
MIDDLE: Nxamaseri Lodge in the Panhandle region offers some of the best birding and fishing in the Okavango Delta.
ABOVE: In many of the camps, boardwalks link the tents to the main dining and lounge complex.

Food for thought

You should never starve on safari. If you're on a budget mobile (see opposite), the food may not set your taste buds alight, but, if you're travelling from lodge to lodge or with a top-end mobile, the food is usually one of the highlights. Some lodges have achieved critical acclaim internationally for serving the finest foods in the most elegant of settings. They will normally feed you three times a day, with a light breakfast in the early morning, a full brunch after the morning game drive, and a three-course dinner in the evening. In between, expect all sorts of snacks to nibble on, with tea and coffee available on tap. Dieters, be warned!

Traditional fare

Mosa Brown, one of the head chefs at Mombo Camp, prepared these traditional recipes (to serve four people).

Seswaa (shredded goat or lamb)

- 4 chopped goat or lamb fillets
- ¾ cup cooking oil
- 2 stock cubes
- salt and pepper

Place all the ingredients in a pot and cover with water. Cook slowly for up to eight hours, until meat is tender and has fallen off the bone. Pound meat with a spoon or rolling pin before serving.

Mosa Brown preparing brunch at Mombo Camp.

Morogo (wild spinach)

- 4 cups water
- 1 kg sliced wild spinach
- 4 tablespoons olive oil
- 1 chopped onion
- garlic to taste
- 1 chopped tomato
- salt and pepper

Bring water to the boil, and then place the spinach in the pot and cook for 15 minutes. Fry the onion with the garlic and add to the pot with the spinach, followed by the tomato, salt and pepper. Cook on a low heat for approximately 30 minutes.

Leputshe (wild pumpkin)

- 500 g pumpkin, peeled and sliced
- 2 tablespoons honey
- 1 teaspoon butter
- salt
- ¼ cup water

Place all the ingredients in the pot and cook over a fire or on the stove over a low heat until ready.

Papa (maize porridge)

- 2 cups water
- salt
- 3 cups maize meal

Pour the water into the pot, add salt and bring to the boil. While stirring, slowly add the maize meal until mixture is a soft porridge. Reduce the heat, leave for 10 minutes, and then stir once more before serving.

The overland experience

Self-drive

Few would argue that Africa is the most exciting continent to cross, and, when all things are considered, Botswana has to be very near the top of the list as the most satisfying country through which to drive. Safe and stable, with an ideal balance of developed infrastructure and wilderness, it's particularly enticing to those who dream of the great overland expedition. Self-drive is about taking the by-roads, the dirt roads and the off-the-beaten-track low roads; it's about feeling the freedom of being out there, but it's also about self-sufficiency and understanding the risks.

The most popular route in Botswana is **Maun to Kasane**, which takes in three of the world's most well-known wildlife destinations: **Moremi**, **Savuti** and **Chobe**. In fact, so popular is it during winter and the South African school holidays, you will most definitely need to book your campsites well in advance (+267-686-1265 or 318-0774). Heading out of Maun via Shorobe, your first stop will be Moremi and one of four campsites: **South Gate**, **Third Bridge**, **Xakanaxa Lagoon** or **North Gate**, which is run by the Department of Wildlife and National Parks (DWNP). All have ablution facilities and water. Next stop will be the only campsite at **Savuti**, the halfway point between Maun and Kasane for overlanders. The last leg leads up to **Chobe National Park**, and can be done either via **Gcoha Hills** and **Kachikau**, or **Nogatsaa** and **Tchinga** in the eastern regions. The main campsite along the Chobe River is no longer at Serondella, the site so familiar to many. It has been moved roughly 15 kilometres west to a site called **Ihaha**. Another option is to camp in one of the many campsites situated outside the park and enter only for game drives. The roads throughout are nothing more than sand tracks, in some cases extremely thick, and during the summer rainy season many become extremely muddy, making driving very difficult.

Other popular self-drive options include the **Makgadikgadi Pans**, the **central Kalahari** and the regions **west of the Panhandle**.

Mobile

Those who love the thrill of the overland safari, yet want the potential headaches of logistical planning taken care of, would do well to book with one of the registered mobile operators. You travel by road, your guide comes with the package and all of your camp equipment follows in back-up vehicles. Like the lodges, a complete range of options is available, but make doubly sure you fully understand what type of trip you have signed on for. Besides the differences in cost, there is also the choice of **'participation'** or **'non-participation'**. Most budget mobiles are participatory, which could mean anything from packing and unpacking the truck daily to peeling the potatoes, and you should expect basic tents with simple food. The other end of the price range is extremely comfortable, with plenty of staff. Don't be surprised if there's even silver and cut-glass tableware! Most mobile safaris are run through the parks and reserves, while some of the up-market operators have exclusive arrangements with private and community concessions.

When on a self-drive safari, always allow a respectful distance between your vehicle and the wildlife.

TOP LEFT: On a self-drive safari you cross the Khwai River Bridge on the way north to Savuti.
TOP RIGHT, AND ABOVE: Game-viewing is best during the dry winter months in Pump Pan, Savuti Marsh.
ABOVE RIGHT: The typical tent used by overland operators.
RIGHT: Wildlife is often seen on the Kasane–Nata Route.
OPPOSITE TOP LEFT: Guests travelling on a top-end overland safari can expect en-suite hot bucket showers.
OPPOSITE TOP RIGHT, MIDDLE LEFT: Public campsite, Savuti Marsh.
OPPOSITE MIDDLE RIGHT: North Gate entrance, Moremi.
OPPOSITE BOTTOM LEFT: North Gate campsite, Moremi.
OPPOSITE BOTTOM RIGHT: On an overland safari all meals are prepared over the open fire.

MOREMI GAME RESERVE
HIPPO POOLS OBSERVATION HIDE &
ABLUTIONS CLOSED FOR REPAIR
STOP

ABOVE: Besides the daily game-viewing rides, guests at Abu Camp also get the opportunity to interact with the elephants while they bath, and during feeding times.
RIGHT: Fly-fishing for tiger fish on the Nxamaseri Channel.

For the adventurous

Not everyone comes for the wildlife. Many come simply for the adventure, and for those adrenalin junkies Botswana has plenty to offer.

Why not start at the traditional end of the spectrum? Rather than doing a single day out on a *mokoro*, spend your full safari at eyeball level with hippo and crocodile, with the added bonus that you also get to spend plenty of time walking. The **Xigera Trail** and **Oddballs** are your best bets, or you could hook up with a mobile operator for a vehicle and *mokoro* combination.

Riding horse and elephant has its own edge: no matter how safe you know it is (and it really is absolutely safe), you can't help having an occasional nervous thought while on another animal's back! Your senses become that much more attuned, which is what the adventure is all about. Before booking a horseback safari in the Okavango, make sure you know how to ride, as they don't take beginners (the horse-riding operation in Mashatu will teach you how to ride). Once you are out there, you need to be able to gallop your way out of trouble. If you pass on all these counts, then five or 10 days riding the floodplains is truly the most exhilarating way to see game. On elephant-back it's a little less vigorous. The attraction here is the unique level of interaction between man and beast, and the leisurely pace allows you to walk alongside these incredible beasts when you're not riding. By the time you have ridden them, walked with them, swum with them, fed them and played a little rough and tumble with the youngsters, there will be nothing you don't know about elephants.

Walking in big game country is another way to fine-tune your senses. Probably because of the terrain, Botswana has in the past not received recognition as a great walking destination. This is changing, though, as more and more operators are offering multi-day walking safaris going from camp to camp (the camps are usually of the more rustic kind). In between walking there will usually be the odd *mokoro* excursion as well. The **Vumbura concession** in the north, and the area around **Pom Pom** and **Xudum** in the south of the Okavango, are fantastic walking areas.

For **fly-fishers**, the tigerfish is the most sought-after of freshwater game fish. There is quite an art to getting them to chase the fly, and, once hooked, they are ferocious fighters that are difficult to keep on the line. The best fly-fishing is in the deeper and faster-flowing waters of the Okavango River in the **Panhandle**.

Mountain bike trails are a hugely successful addition to the list of adventure options offered by Mashatu Game Reserve.

Hippo channels are often the most convenient routes to follow when crossing extensive wetland areas by *mokoro*.

Be guided

So, you've taken care in selecting your preferred wilderness area, the season in which to travel and your favourite lodges and camps, but what about the person who is going to be essential in making your safari a once-in-a-lifetime trip? Don't forget to ask about your guide! An exciting safari experience depends as much on the guide you are with as it does on any other element of your trip. Great guides can turn an ordinary lodge or an uneventful game drive into the thrill of a lifetime.

All the guides have undergone training of some sort, and those from the larger and more reputable operators will also have completed courses on rifle training and first aid treatment. Regular visitors will know exactly whom they want but, if you're on your first safari, give as precise a description of your interests as possible when booking, and the chances are you'll end up with someone who can meet your expectations.

There are many guides who have earned notable reputations. In the course of a standard safari you'll have a different guide at each lodge you visit, but some operators do offer the services of specialist guides, who accompany their guests throughout their safari.

Approaching plains game species on foot is an awesome experience. Be sure, though, to listen to your guide's instructions at all times.

JULIUS MASOGA ▶▶

With his trademark smile and jovial manner, the 'Galloping Horse', as he is known to his many repeat guests, has become a fixture at Mombo Camp, from where he has been guiding over the last 10 years. Few other guides know the region as Julius does, ensuring him more than his fair share of prime sightings – particularly when it comes to his favourite species, the leopard. He has, over the years, also become known to guests as the leader in the local Mombo Choir, a position he owes to a fine sense of humour and his sociable nature.

◀◀ MIKE PENMAN

Larger-than-life Mike is possibly the best known of Botswana's professional guides, a reputation he has earned from leading trips in his inimitable and thrilling way over the last 20 years. His regular appearances in numerous wildlife documentaries featuring him as both commentator and lead have also helped to make him a household name within the safari industry. Mike has a fascination with lions, and built his reputation tracking the large cats in the Kwando and Linyanti regions before he moved to the Okavango over 10 years ago. Under the banner of Wild Lifestyles, Mike and his partner Angie now operate their own overland operation throughout the Okavango and parts of the Central Kalahari. They received the ultimate accolade in 2002 when Condé Nast *Traveler* magazine voted their operation one of the top 15 overland outfits in the world.

SPENCER MATHAMBO ▶▶

Hailing from the eastern regions of Botswana, Spencer began his life in the wilds as a guide in the Tuli Block, close to his home village, before moving to the Okavango. After stints at Abu and a number of other camps, he moved north to the Kwando Concession where he has been based at Lebala Camp for the last three years. For him, there is no more rewarding a region in which to be guiding, and he does not see himself moving in the years to come. His interests include the cats and the resident pack of wild dogs. Spencer is the senior guide on the concession.

◀◀ FRANK MASHEBE

Frank grew up in Kasane in Botswana's far north-east, in a family that has always been involved in the tourism industry. With his father and older brothers all career guides, there was no dilemma for him when it came to deciding on his own future. He began taking guests into the Chobe National Park in the mid-1990s, before moving to the Jao region of the Delta in 1999. His name has become synonymous with this concession, where he is the senior guide and part of the top management team. His charming and urbane manner has made him a firm favourite with return guests and one of the most popular guides amongst his peers. While he leads all types of trips, Frank's knowledge and enthusiastic appreciation of the smaller creatures and less obvious aspects of the wilderness make him one of the finest guides to be with on a walking safari.

BK BALOI ▶▶

With a science degree in biology from Botswana University, BK is one of a new generation of citizen guides joining the safari industry. BK is also fond of being with people, so for him it was a natural progression to use his qualification as a professional guide rather than as a scientist, although he does not count out the possibility of returning to the academic world at a later stage. His first love is the remote central regions of the country and particularly the Makgadikgadi Pans. Based at Jack's Camp, BK can be found leading quad bike trips and explaining the finer ecological aspects of the pans and their wildlife, as well as the region's rich archaeological history.

◀◀ PJ BESTELINK

A doyen of the Okavango's earlier days, PJ is one of only a few from that era who have successfully adapted to the changing demands of the present tourism climate. He first came to northern Botswana in the 1960s as a field geologist looking for mineral deposits, but discovered the Okavango instead. That was the end of his former profession, as he stayed to embark on what has become a lifelong enchantment with the Delta. Over the years PJ built three camps, all of which continue to thrive today, before he and his wife Barney pioneered horseback safaris in the late 1980s. Today they run a world-renowned operation from their camp Kujwana in the southern regions of the Okavango. Recognised as one of the most experienced field guides in Botswana, PJ is also known as a being a fly-fisherman of note, a hobby he pursues with dedicated passion.

ISHMAEL SETLABOSHA ▶▶

With over 20 years of poling experience, Ish is considered one of the finest *mokoro* guides in the Okavango. This is hardly surprising, as he was born on Jedibe Island in the north-western reaches of the Delta where poling a dugout is the only way to get around. One of four brothers, all well-known guides, Ish decided in the early 1990s to specialise in the most traditional of safari options. He has spent most of his professional guiding career with Okavango Wilderness Safaris and has been based at Xigera for the last few years, where he leads the camp's three-night *mokoro* trails. A trip with Ish is a magical way to explore the wonders of the waterways, and when around the evening campfire be sure to ask about his close encounter with a lion that so very nearly got the better of him during his youth.

◀◀ PETER HOLBROW

With 22 years of experience gained in hunting throughout southern Africa, Peter is one of Botswana's most respected professional hunters. Having grown up on a game farm in South Africa, a career involving wildlife was always going to be his destiny. He qualified as a professional hunter soon after leaving school and hunted in South Africa, Zimbabwe and Zambia before moving to Botswana in the early 1990s. Holbrow Hunting Safaris operates from Selby's Camp, within a large private concession in the south-western reaches of the Okavango. Peter offers a chance to hunt all the big game species, as well as bird shooting, and, given a choice, will always use a *mokoro* as his mode of transport for hunting.

wildlife WONDERS

Driven by thirst, elephants will often quicken their pace as they approach a water hole. Adults can drink up to 100 litres at a time, and may drink over 200 litres in a 24-hour cycle.

The diverse array of wildlife and the natural enviroments in which it is found are the major drawcard for visitors to southern Africa. Botswana is home to a wonderful range of animal species and habitats, and is for many the most rewarding of the safari destinations within the region. Its natural heritage includes almost 550 different bird species, over 170 mammal, 150 reptile, 40 amphibian and 80 fish species, as well as over 3 000 recorded plant species, all ensuring that a trip through any of the country's many wilderness areas can't fail to impress.

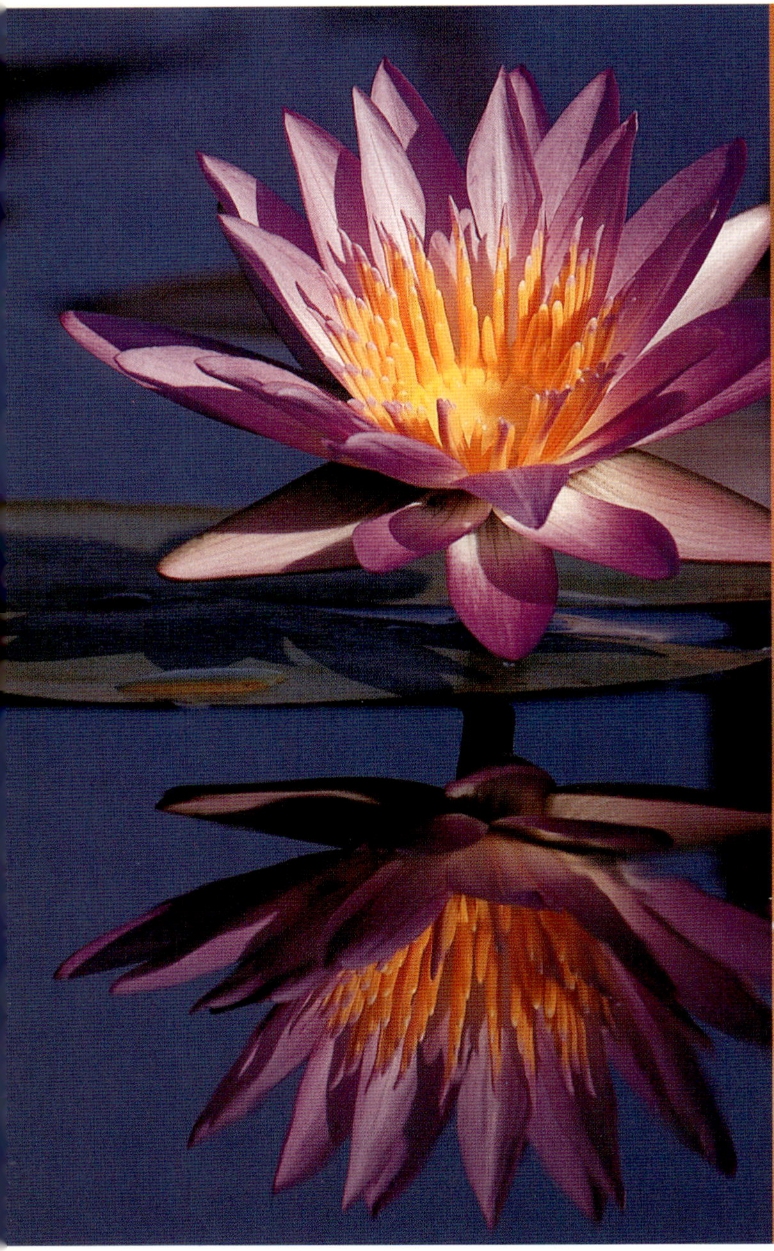
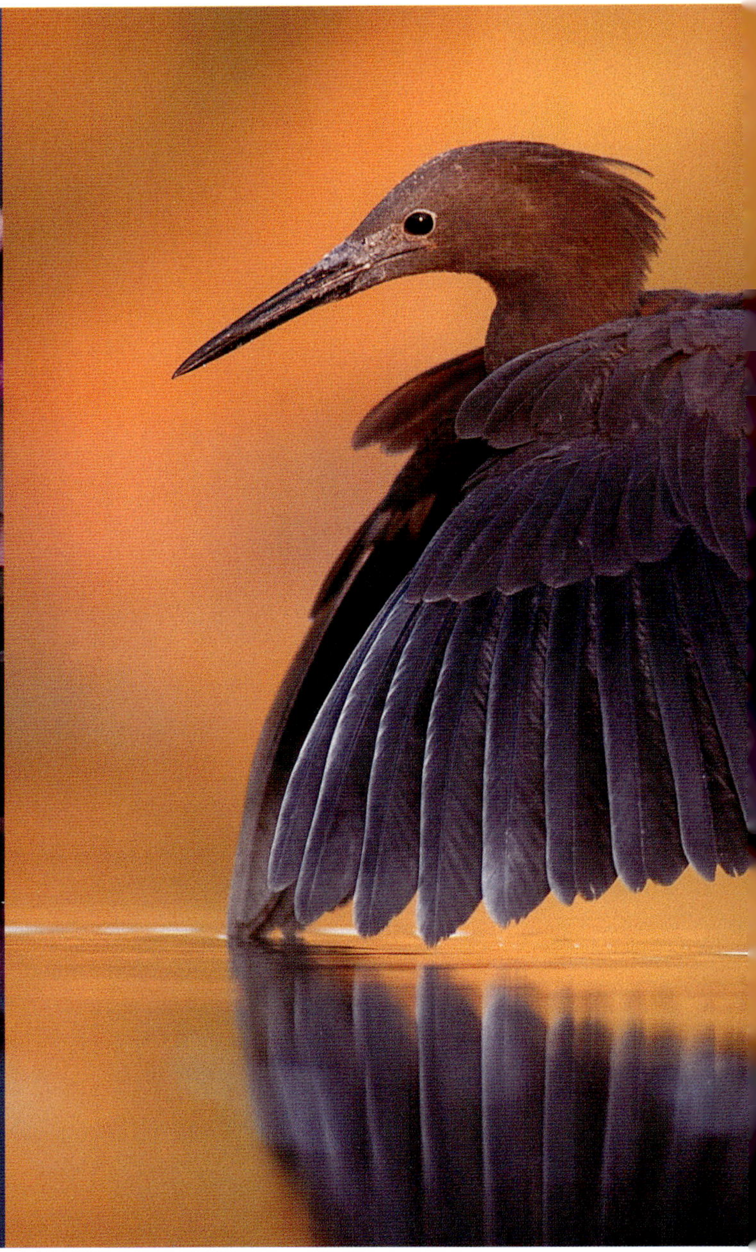

Birdlife

OPPOSITE LEFT: The root rhizome of the water lily (*Nymphaea nouchali*) provides a source of nutritious food for the people of the Panhandle. They are dug out from below the water and eaten either raw or roasted.
LEFT: The black egret has a unique feeding behaviour known as shading. By using the wings to cover its head, it creates a canopy of shade that is thought to attract small fish and other aquatic organisms.
ABOVE: For birders the Pel's fishing owl is a prize tick on their must-see list. It is not so much scarce as difficult to spot, and the best way to find it is to look amongst the densest of trees on heavily wooded islands.

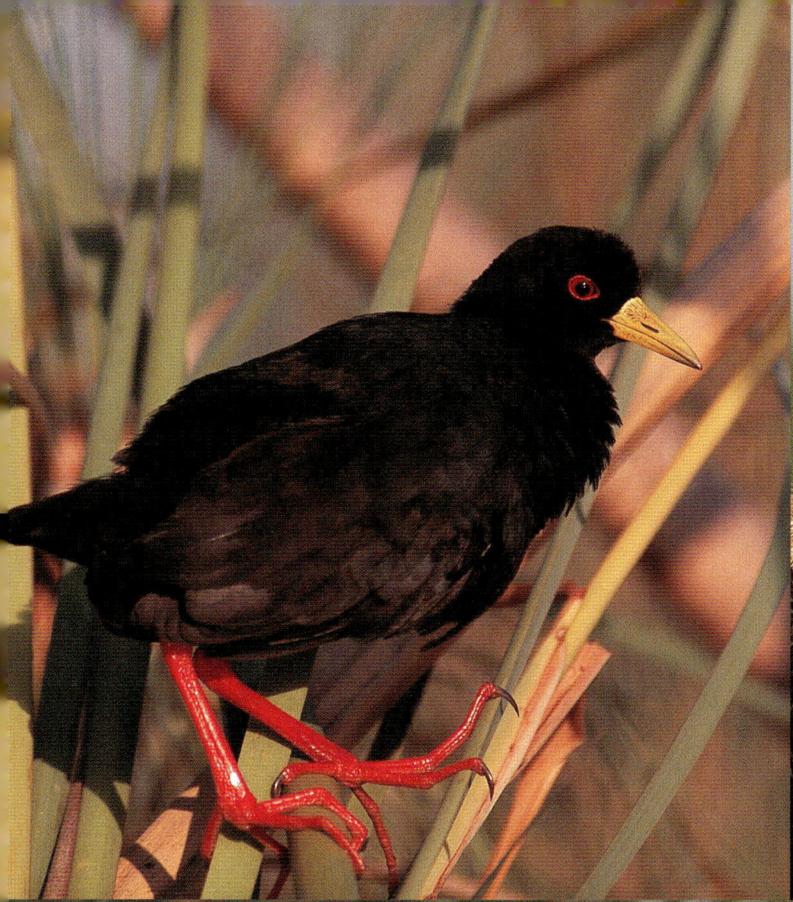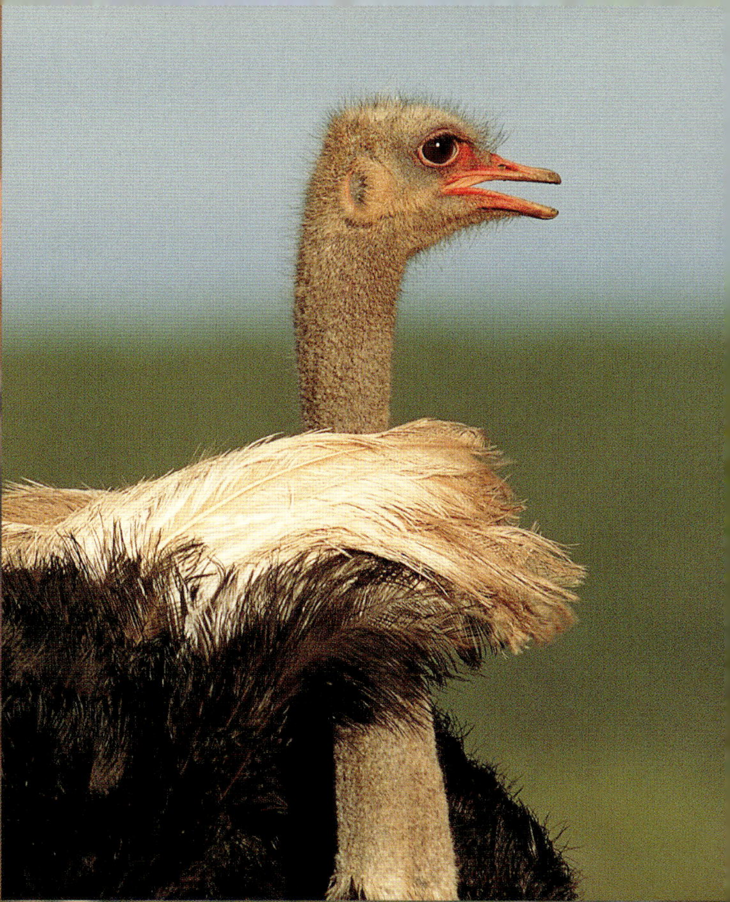
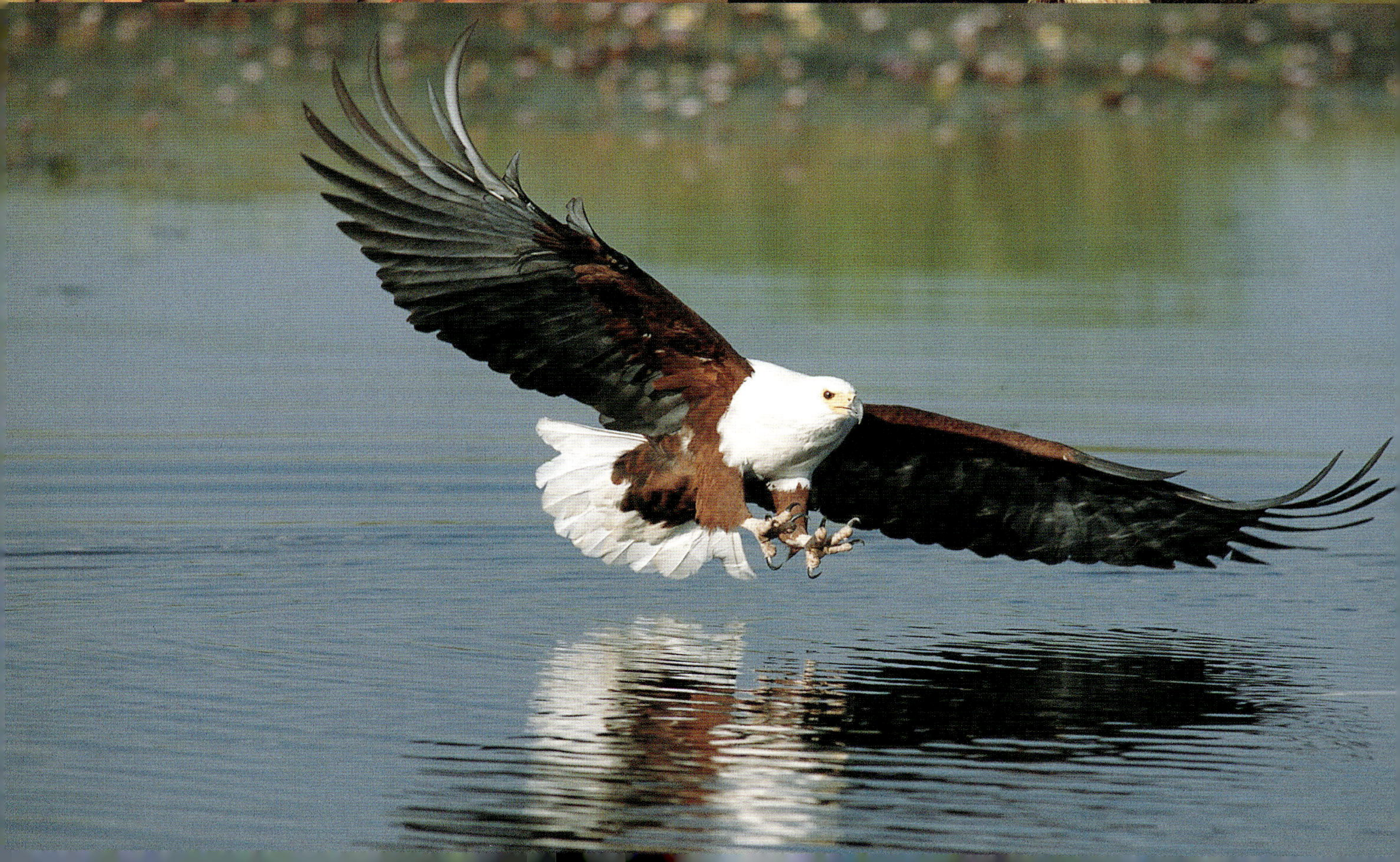

Opposite top left: Black crake are commonly seen scrambling about the lower levels in papyrus beds on all waterways and lagoons throughout the Okavango Delta.
Opposite top right: Male ostriches raise their wings and swirl them about above the body in a mating display, to attract female suitors.
Opposite bottom, and below: There is nothing more majestic than a fish eagle sweeping down to grab a fish from just below the water's surface. These birds are commonly seen throughout Botswana, wherever there is permanent water. (The photograph below was a set-up with a dead fish thrown for the fish eagle.)
Top left: This female bateleur shows the adult plumage colours that make her the most striking of all raptors. While these birds are not common, visitors on an extended safari should be able to see them, particularly in the drier regions.
Left: Common throughout the Okavango Delta and the waterways of Chobe and Linyanti, little bee-eaters have a habit of huddling together at favourite roost sites during the cold winter months.

Animal portraits

Lions are usually on the top of 'must-see' lists. While they occur in every national park and in most private concessions, the best viewing is in the central and northern regions of the Okavango and in the Moremi, the Savuti Marsh and along the Linyanti, Kwando and Chobe rivers.

Roan antelope are on the endangered list in southern Africa. For the best chances of viewing them, visit the drier camps in the Chobe, Linyanti and Kwando regions, and the far northern Okavango during winter.

TOP LEFT: Warthog, which have been known to share their burrows with nocturnal species such as hyena, have the habit of reversing into the entrance so that their heads always face whatever danger may be lurking.
ABOVE LEFT: The silhouette of a leopard cleaning itself – something they do on a regular basis, but particularly after feeding.
ABOVE RIGHT: Being predominately a nocturnal species, and because of their solitary and secretive nature, leopards are not seen nearly as often as lions. However, once habituated to the game drive vehicles, they offer exciting close-up photographic opportunities. An extremely adaptable species, they are found in almost every type of terrain.

Male giraffe engage in a form of combat known as necking. The animals stand side by side and swing their heads in order to land hefty blows on each other's neck and upper chest. This behaviour will eventually determine the hierarchy of dominance amongst the adults.

Predators

Of the large cat species, leopards have the most varied and adaptable diets. In the areas where medium-sized and smaller antelope species, such as impala and steenbok, occur, these form the majority of the leopard's prey. In more marginal areas, they will prey on birds, rodents and even carrion.

ABOVE: Lions commonly form coalitions, usually with two or three members but occasionally with as many as four or five, which improves their chances of holding a pride territory for longer periods. Here two lions share a buffalo kill, but with smaller carcasses they will often compete aggressively for food.

LEFT: Wild dogs hunt in packs, and small- and medium-sized antelope are their favoured prey. Once an animal has been brought down, the dogs feed together and, if there are pups with the pack, they are allowed to eat before the adults.

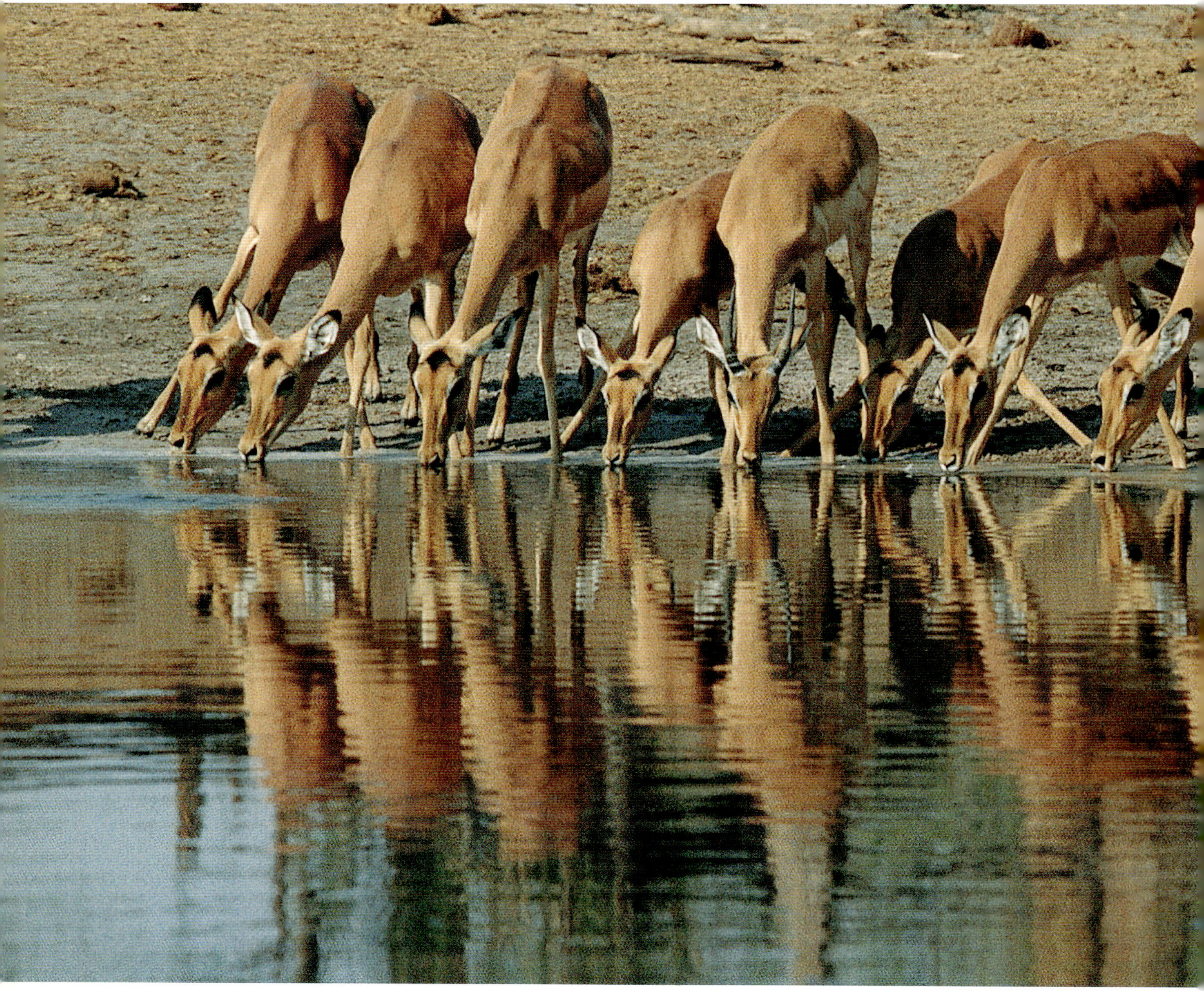

The plains game

Taut with tension, a group of impala drink at a water hole: they are particularly vulnerable from attack by predators when they are drinking.

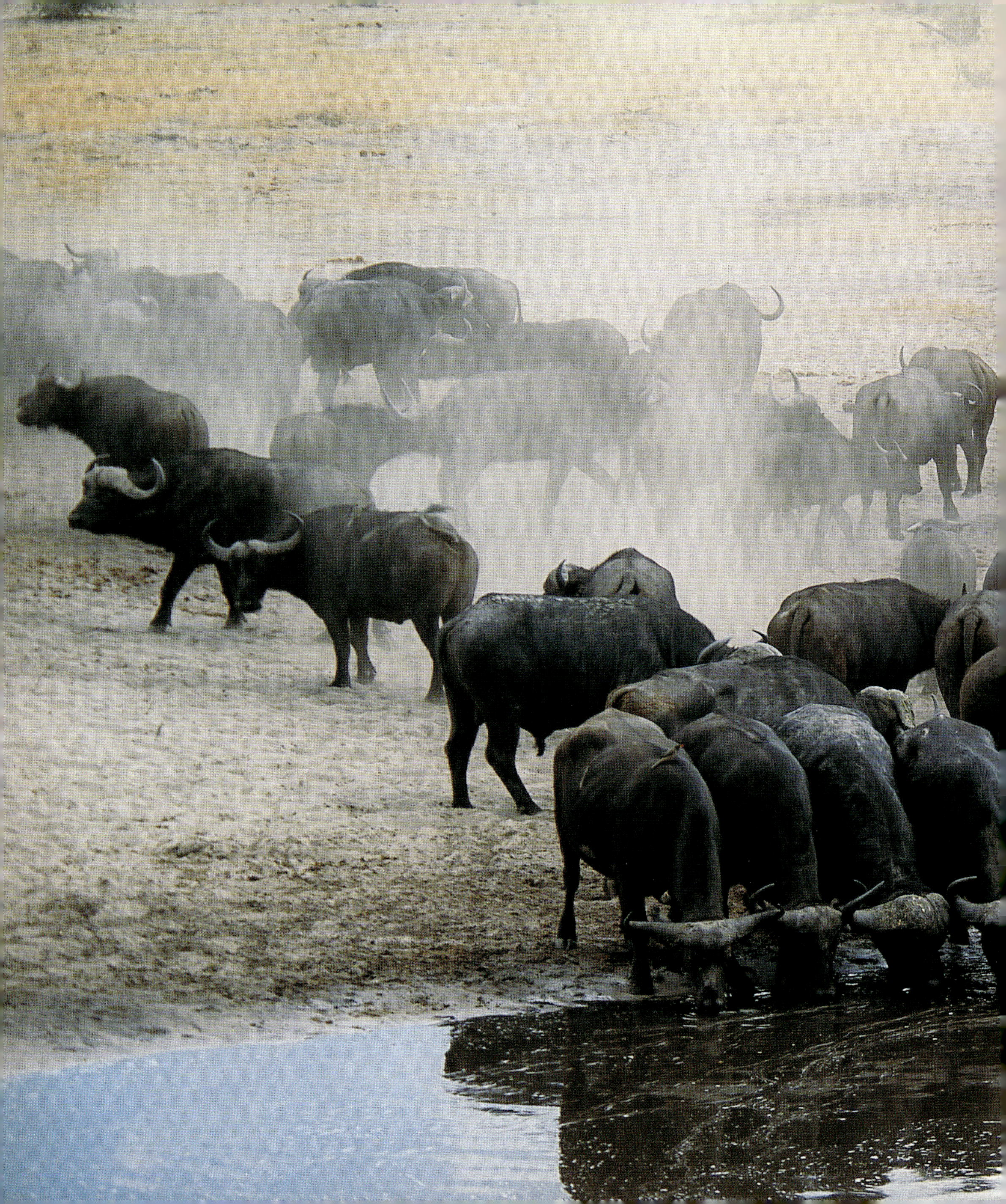

Buffalo are highly gregarious, non-territorial animals and have large home ranges. Although an average-sized herd consists of several hundred animals, in the northern areas of the Okavango Delta and the Chobe National Park they move in herds of over a thousand.

Adult elephants need on average to consume in excess of 180 kilograms of food every day. During the dry winter months, when food becomes scarce, they will regularly cross the Linyanti and Chobe rivers between Botswana and Namibia in search of better feeding grounds.

Of all the antelope species, the red lechwe has the strongest association with the waters of the Okavango. Adaptations, including long, splayed hooves, strong hindquarters and a shaggy coat, allow them to inhabit the islands and floodplain edges wherever water occurs.

Plants & trees

RIGHT: The unmistakable shape and colour of the fireball lily (*Scadoxus multiflorus*) appears in mixed woodland once the first rains have fallen. Both the bulbs and leaves of this plant are highly toxic.
BELOW: Mature umbrella thorns (*Acacia tortilis*) can reach over 20 metres in height. The semi-circular pods are highly nutritious, making them a favourite food source for elephants and many of the plains game species.

Many of the islands in the central and northern Okavango Delta are dominated by the two palm species found in the region. The taller real fan palm (*Hyphaene petersiana*, seen here in the foreground) grows in the drier central sections of the island, and the wild date palm (*Phoenix reclinata*, in the background) thrives around the wetter island fringes.

Delta blues

Despite its uniqueness and prominent ecological standing, including being recognised as the planet's largest and most significant Ramsar Wetland Site, the Okavango Delta is afforded no special protection. As a result, there are a number of serious threats to its long-term existence. In fact, certain conservation bodies already consider the extended wildlife ecosystem of northern Botswana to be **critically endangered**. While some of these issues are of a localised nature, giving them a reasonable chance of being resolved by the various stakeholders, those that are more ominous concern Namibia and Angola, and are likely to require a concerted international effort. Recommendations and proposals have been put forward to have the region declared a World Heritage Site. It is hoped that this move would ensure its future protection and survival. In the meantime, both local and international conservation agencies should not for one moment relax their vigilance.

Disruption of the water flow

The most serious threat to the Delta, and one that could be catastrophic, is the construction of any form of **dam or weir**, particularly if built in **Namibia or Angola**, that would disrupt the flow of water and sediment load that enters the Delta on an annual basis. In 1991 mining interests within Botswana proposed to divert the Okavango's waters via a number of canals that were to be dredged north of Maun, but, with the help of international conservation agencies, the people of Ngamiland managed to halt the potentially devastating scheme. It would be naïve to assume that more such initiatives are not likely to arise in the future. The biggest threat is likely to come from Angola, as, after decades of civil war, the people are now looking to rebuild their country and dams may very well be on the agenda.

Commercial cattle ranching

Outside of **Ngamiland**, Botswana is mostly cattle country. And, as the rangelands of the southern and central regions become degraded from **overgrazing and overstocking**, the relatively untouched communal lands surrounding the Okavango are beginning to look ever more enticing to the powerful cattle lobby. Rezoning this wildlife region into a commercial cattle zone would herald an invasion of livestock and the erection of more veterinary fences, which would end the seasonal use of ancient migratory routes by certain herbivore species. Predator control measures would, in all likelihood, also be stepped up. The end result would be that the Okavango becomes like most other wilderness areas on the continent: a national park totally surrounded by human and commercial activity. With the demise of free-ranging wildlife populations, Botswana would lose the competitive advantage that it presently enjoys in southern Africa as the most special of safari destinations.

Commercial gill netting

Worldwide, gill netting has been either banned or heavily restricted, but not in the Okavango Delta. This is a legacy of previous misguided attempts by aid agencies to provide rural communities with the means to get more protein, and the Panhandle and certain regions within the community areas of the Delta are now literally littered with gill nets. Operating with impunity and, in some instances using nets that are a few hundred metres in length, the commercial fishermen will in time plunder the Okavango's fish resources if left unregulated. **Catfish and various bream species** are the major fish being harvested, with the bream going mostly to supermarkets, restaurants and lodges, and the catfish to village markets.

Other important issues in the Delta:

▶▶ The **uncontrolled and illegal lighting of fires** that annually burn over 30 percent of the Okavango and environs.

▶▶ The **unprofessional and illegal hunting practices** that can have an impact on the numbers and the gene pools of certain species on the trophy lists.

▶▶ Although not yet an issue, excessive pressures being brought to bear on the environment from **tourism** may very well become a problem in the future.

Above: There are almost 2.5 million head of cattle in Botswana. As it is mostly a semi-arid country, over 100 000 square kilometres in the central and southern regions have already been degraded in some form because of overgrazing.
Left: Gill nets are indiscriminate in what they kill, with otters, small crocodiles and water birds often becoming entangled.
Below: Once alight and fed by the highly inflammable reed and papyrus beds, uncontrolled fires can burn for weeks on end. They are most often started by reed and grass cutters and commercial gill-net fishermen.

Science & conservation at work

Numerous scientific researchers and fieldworkers are involved in various projects throughout the national parks, reserves and wildlife management areas. Mostly unsung and often working under trying conditions, these dedicated people are involved in ongoing research and monitoring programmes that are crucial to the **conservation of Botswana's biodiversity**. Anyone wishing to get involved, as a volunteer or to assist with financial aid, may contact any of the following projects or groups:

Baboon Research – Robert Seyforth: baboon@sratosnet.com

BirdLife Botswana (Projects on various species) – Pete Hancock: pete@info.bw

Botswana Crane Working Group – Sekgowa Motsumi: cranegroup@dynabyte.bw

Botswana Wild Dog Research Project – Tico McNutt or Megan Parker: 2bwdrp@bushmail.net

Elephant Research – Mike Chase: er@info.bw

Lion Research (Xudum region of the Okavango) – Christiaan or Hanlie Winterbach: ensign@dynabyte.bw

Makgadikgadi Brown Hyaena Research Project – Glenn Maude or Ross Burrough: brownhyaena@info.bw

Makgadikgadi Lion Research – Seamus Maclennan: ensign@dynabyte.bw

Makgadikgadi Zebra Research – Chris Brooks: ensign@dynabyte.bw

Okavango Lion Research Program (Santawani region of the Okavango) – Pieter Kat: panthera.leo@dynabyte.bw

Okavango Research Centre – Prof. Lars Ramberg: hoorc@orc.ub.bw

In the northern regions, wild animals can be seen along all the major roads. Be watchful, and don't speed.

The following is a list of conservation organisations and wildlife societies active in Botswana:

Conservation International – Private Bag 132, Maun, tel: +267-686-0017, email: cibots@info.bw, website: www.conservation.org

Chobe Wildlife Trust – PO Box 55, Kasane, tel: +267-625-0516, email: cwt@info.bw

Kalahari Conservation Society – PO Box 859, Gaborone, tel: +267-397-4557, email: kcs@botsnet.bw

Khama Rhino Sanctuary – PO Box 10, Serowe, tel: +267-463-0713, email: krst@botsnet.bw

Mokolodi Wildlife Foundation – PO Box 170, Gaborone, tel: +267-596-1955/6, email: mokolodi@info.bw

The Mombo Rhino Introduction Programme – Private Bag 14, Maun, tel: +267-686-0086, email: grantw@ows.bw

Morama Wildlife Reserve – Private Bag 14, Maun, tel: +267-724-3760, email: chrisk@ows.bw

BirdLife Botswana – Private Bag 13, Gaborone, tel: +267-686-5618, email: blb@birdlifebotswana.org.bw

Bana Banaga or Children in the Wilderness – Private Bag 14, Maun, tel: +267-686-0086, email: chrisk@ows.bw

Somarelang Tikologo – Private Bag 00376, Gaborone, tel: +267-391-3709, email: somatiko@info.bw

Rhino can now be seen in the Okavango for the first time in over twenty years, thanks to a successful reintroduction programme carried out by the Department of Wildlife and National Parks and Wilderness Safaris.

out of the WAY

So much of Botswana's appeal lies in the wide-open spaces and the fact that there are still so many out-of-the-way places (long may it stay that way). However, rapid growth rates, new roads and improving telecommunications are making almost everywhere that much more accessible. Until very recently it took a back-breaking three hours to reach Tsodilo Hills, just 40 kilometres off the main road, and now it's an easy 30 minutes. The road south from Maun to Ghanzi was a hellish four hours a few years back, but, with the new tarred road, it's a breeze at one hour and twenty minutes or so. Nonetheless, there is still plenty of wilderness out there for you to get lost in and where you can just soak up the silence and solitude.

Remember, when doing these trips you will need to be self-sufficient, particularly with regards to water and fuel supplies. Villages along the way may have rudimentary supplies only. It is also recommended, when going through parts of the Central Kalahari and to the north-east of the Okavango, that you travel in a group of at least two 4x4 vehicles.

The Central Kalahari

This is where you go for the 'great escape', and the longer you spend here the less you will feel like returning. This is big sky country at its most remote, with every chance that you may not bump into another soul. And the experiences that you can have here are unique – seeing black-maned lions, barking geckos, pronking springbok and blood red sunsets that match the colour of the shallow dunes. **The Central Kalahari Game Reserve**, originally proclaimed to protect the traditional hunting rights of the Bushmen, covers almost 53 000 square kilometres of semi-arid grassland, sparse acacia woodland and dry fossil riverbeds. Add the 2 590-square-kilometre **Khutse Game Reserve**, which shares a boundary to the south, and you have one of the largest protected areas anywhere on the planet pretty much to yourself.

Access is off the Nata–Maun road along the Makalamabedi cutline. From Maun, it should take you a little over four hours to reach the reserve. Alternative entry points are from Rakops (ask for directions in the village) and through Khutse from the Gaborone side. This road goes via the small town of Letlhakeng, but fill up at Molepolole as this is the last fuel station. Both the Central Kalahari and Khutse have a number of designated campsites, most of which have no facilities, and don't bank on water being available either! Another option is to use the **Deception Valley Lodge** (+ 27-12-346-6864) as your base. The lodge is situated just outside the reserve's northern boundary, and access to it is also along the cutline. It was Mark and Delia Owens who brought Deception to the attention of the world with tales of their life and work in the book *Cry of the Kalahari*.

Because of the arid conditions, game in these regions is usually scattered, but there are times during the summer months when local migrations take place and, during the early winter period, you may find animals concentrating around the remaining waterholes. Otherwise, ask wildlife officials at the entry gates about which pans are being artificially pumped, and head for those. World renowned for their majestic black-maned lions, these parks also offer reasonable numbers of oryx, springbok, eland, red hartebeest and ostrich. Cheetah, giraffe, wildebeest, brown hyena and many of the smaller species can also be seen, but less regularly.

The Kgalagadi Transfrontier Park

Many will know this protected area as the **Gemsbok National Park**. It made history by being the first fully operational transfrontier park on the continent, when it opened its gates in May 2000. It's now run as a combined unit with the **Mabuasehube Game Reserve** and the South African **Kalahari Gemsbok National Park**, and consists of almost 38 000 square kilometres of desert-like dunes and grassland – not too dissimilar to the Central Kalahari. The Gemsbok side of the park has a variety of accommodation and campsites, while Mabuasehube has more rudimentary camping only. The best access is from the South African side via Bokspits. Be warned, though, that entry through the South African side of the park does not allow you entry into the Botswanan side unless you have booked your campsites. Entry via Mabuasehube is more testing. Two heavy sand tracks, one heading south from Tshane and the other north from Tshabong, are your alternatives. The best game viewing is along the Nossob and Auob river valleys where lion, cheetah, oryx, springbok, red hartebeest and eland are commonly seen. The raptor viewing during the summer months is among the most rewarding to be found anywhere in southern Africa.

The opposite side of the Okavango

It's not often included as a destination, but the eastern bank of the Okavango River makes for a terrific trip away from the beaten tar, and particularly so for those who are fascinated by rural village life. Cross the **Okavango River by ferry** (it's the only one on the river) a short distance north of Shakawe, and just follow the dirt road all along the eastern bank of the river. Stop in any or all of the villages and spend time with the people for the most authentic of cross-cultural interactions. **Seronga** and **Ganitsuga** have community campsites with basic facilities, or just ask to camp wherever you find yourself. For those wanting a comfortable bed ask at Seronga for directions to **Modumo Lodge** (+267-680-0880), and the chance for some game viewing as well. The **Okavango Polers Trust**, a community-based operation in Serongo, will be able to provide *mokoro* polers and guides for you, if you want to spend time on the waterways. If you're feeling really intrepid, push on through **Eretse and Betsha** and link up with the Maun–Chobe road, or head north to the Kwando region. Once you've left the villages this is real lonely countryside, so be well prepared.

The Aha Hills and Gcwihaba Cave

Lying within 27 kilometres of each other, south of Tsodilo Hills, these two sites are located in one of the more remote corners of the country, close to the Namibian border. The turnoff is at **Nokaneng**, along the western edge of the Okavango. What used to be at least a five-hour battle through deep sand has become a quicker and more sedate ride on a recently graded dirt road. Aha consists of two large limestone and dolomite hills, which you may want to scramble up, before heading on to the cave. But first, for the sake of eco-tourism and your safety, it's worth stopping at the tiny village of **Xai-Xai** almost 10 kilometres past the hills to hire the services of a local Bushman guide.

The **Gcwihaba Cave**, which is a national monument, is situated at the base of a collection of rocky outcrops alongside an old fossil riverbed. There are north and south entrances, which do meet somewhere amidst the caverns inside, but let your guide choose the way in, and make sure you take a number of flashlights or lanterns as it is extremely dark. The best wildlife is to be found on the cave ceilings above you, usually in the centre somewhere, where reasonable numbers of slit-faced and leaf-nosed bats can be seen roosting. If you are travelling with two or more vehicles, you can try the alternative route back to Maun following the narrow sand track that heads out past the Gcwihaba Hills.

ABOVE: The load of freshly cut papyrus on this Bayei woman's head will be used to make rudimentary matting.
BELOW: During the summer months, large herds of zebra migrate into the Central Kalahari to take advantage of the fresh grasses that begin growing once the first summer rains have fallen. The best viewing is at water holes such as this one at Meno A Kwena Camp on the way to the Central Kalahari Game Reserve.

A roadside pot market on the Selebi Phikwe–Serule road.

ART
for all

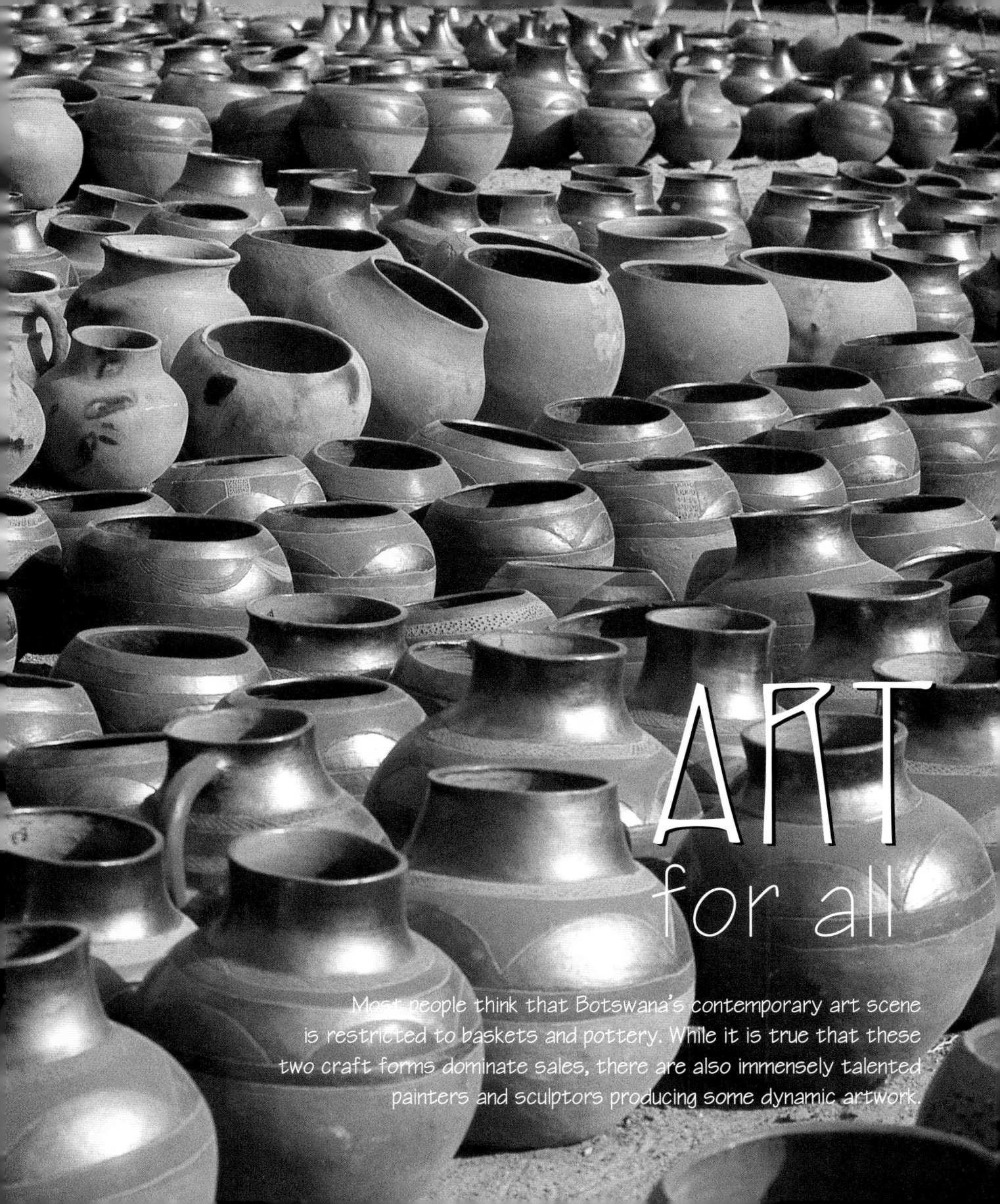

Most people think that Botswana's contemporary art scene is restricted to baskets and pottery. While it is true that these two craft forms dominate sales, there are also immensely talented painters and sculptors producing some dynamic artwork.

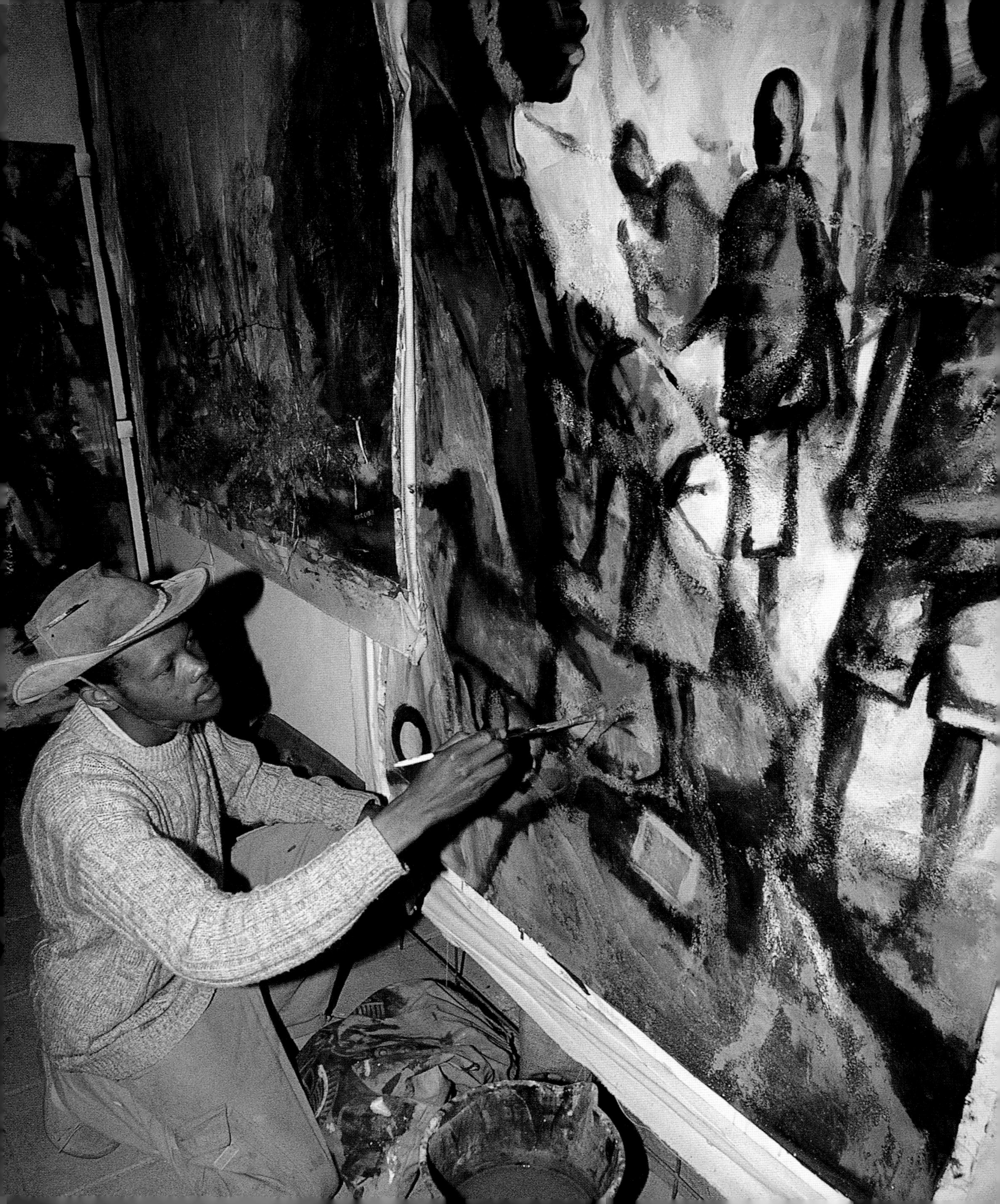

Check out the galleries or organisations below for Botswana's best paintings, photography and sculpture. Look out, in particular, for the creations of **Isaac Chibua (pictured painting opposite)** and **Brad Bestelink**, two local artists who are creating a buzz with their exciting work.

In Gaborone:
- Gallery Ann
- Octagon Gallery, in the National Museum
- Frame Gallery
- Thapong Visual Arts Centre
- The African Easel

In Maun:
- Nhabe Museum
- African Art and Images

Pottery

Traditionally, clay pots were used as an integral part of daily life, so making the step to crafting them as a commercial enterprise is a simple one. Clay pots are used for storing water and traditional beer, and also for cooking. Traditionally, the women within the community are responsible for collecting and moulding the clay, with the most sought-after clays being the kaolin-based ones that produce red and brown colours. Once the form of the pot has been created, decorative patterns are added using natural oxides. Today, pots are produced mainly in the south and east of the country, where the best clay soils occur. There are commercial pottery centres in **Thamaga**, **Molepolole**, **Kanye** and **Gaborone**.

Wooden crafts

Wooden crafts are produced throughout Botswana, but the **Hambukushu** and **Basubiya** people are the most renowned as artists. Products such as kitchen utensils, chairs, drums, thumb pianos and knives are commonly sold along the roadside or in the craft co-operatives that are found in most villages and towns. The Hambukushu in northern Botswana are well known for their more artistic carvings, particularly of animals, and for the simple yet distorted style of their human figurines. The craft centres and shops in **Gaborone**, **Ghanzi**, **Gumare**, **Serowe**, **Maun**, **Francistown** and **Kasane** sell a good variety of wooden arts and crafts.

Bushman art

The earliest artists were the Bushman people, masters of rock painting and supreme crafters, using either wood, leather or ostrich shell. Today, commercial products – based on the traditional forms of their bows and arrows used for hunting, their loin cloths, leather bags and beaded necklaces – can be bought in most co-operative outlets, found throughout Botswana. Bushman artists have also more recently begun to achieve success with their very distinctive style of painting. Bright and full of human and animal images, the pieces mostly depict the deep connections their lifestyles have to nature. If you find yourself travelling the Trans-Kalahari Highway to Maun, be sure to stop off in the tiny village of **D'Kar** (about 30 kilometres outside Ghanzi), as the craft gallery here usually has some amazing works on offer.

The Botswana National Museum

This is the multi-disciplinary institution that acts as custodian of Botswana's cultural and natural heritage. The assets under their care include the **National Art Gallery**, the **Octagon Gallery**, the **National Library**, the **Botswana National Museum** and 78 national monuments spread across the country. The museum also has various mobile outreach programmes, which aim to 'take the museum to the public', and a weekly radio programme that 'tells of the oral traditions of the people of Botswana'. The art galleries host exhibitions by some of Africa's finest contemporary artists, and the various museum galleries and archives have extensive natural and historical collections. The museum's main campus is situated in Gaborone, near the Main Mall and opposite the Catholic cathedral. For further information visit: www.botswana-museum.gov.bw or national.museum@gov.bw

---

OPPOSITE: Isaac Chibua, who is one of Botswana's up-and-coming artists, works on a canvas from his studio at the Thapong Visual Arts Centre in the capital city Gaborone. His work is on display here and in a number of galleries in Gaborone.

Bushman artists have recently begun to achieve success with their very distinctive style of painting. Bright and full of human and animal images, the pieces mostly depict the deep connections their lifestyles have with nature.

Traditional dancing displays are put on in most of the safari camps.

Slow and intricate work: a large basket, like this one being woven by a Bayei woman, can take up to two weeks to complete.

Baskets of Botswana

Botswana is synonymous with the subcontinent's most intricate and beautifully woven baskets, made mostly by the **Bayei** and **Hambukushu** women from the north-western regions of the Okavango Delta. These woven artifacts have, for hundreds of years, been an essential component of village life for these people. Traditionally, closed baskets with lids are used as storage containers for a variety of grains and seeds, as well as sorghum beer (*boljalwa*); tray-type and bowl baskets, which are carried by women on their heads, are for more general use.

All the baskets are made from the leaf fibre of the young real fan palm (*Hyphaene petersiana*) or *mokolwane* in Setswana, which gets stripped into strings before weaving. Nearly all baskets have a pattern of some type woven into the bodywork and, to obtain coloured fibre, the palm strings are pounded and then soaked in a boiling solution of natural dyes taken from the bark and roots of various plants. Reds are extracted from the bird plum (*Berchemia discolor*), browns from the magic guarri (*Euclea divinorum*), purples from the indigo dye plant (*Indigofera tinctoria* and *arrecta*) and yellows from the red star apple (*Diospyros lyciodes*).

The traditional designs on baskets consisted of a few patterns that portrayed the natural world and were produced using few colours. They went by such poetic names as 'Flight of the Swallows', 'Urine Trail of the Bull', 'Tears of the Giraffe', 'Knees of the Tortoise' and 'Forehead of the Zebra'. While these designs are still used in the rural areas, most baskets are now produced for the commercial market – in a number of new shapes, sizes, colours and modern patterns that have been introduced.

Basketware, sold mostly through co-operatives, has become an important source of supplementary income for many rural families. For the very best baskets, stop off in the villages of **Nxamaseri**, **Sepopa**, **Etsha 13** and **Etsha 6**, and just ask at the nearest hut where to buy baskets.

A collection of baskets displaying vivid colours and patterns.

the life and
SOUL

Proud, strong-willed and resourceful, the people of Botswana are certainly the life and soul of their country and the major reason for Botswana's successes over the last century.

A Bayei bridal procession heads for the groom's family home, where the marriage ceremony will take place. The bride, third from the front, is always dressed in white.

The people

Who's who

All of the citizens of Botswana are collectively referred to as Batswana (plural form) or Motswana (singular form), and can be grouped into two broad categories: the Setswana-speaking people and the non-Setswana-speakers. Over 60 percent of the population traces their heritage to one of the Setswana-speaking groups:

▶▶ The **Bangwato**, who constitute the largest of the Setswana-speaking groups, come from Serowe.

▶▶ The **Bakgatla**, **Bakwena**, **Barolong** and **Bangwaketse** come from the southern regions around Gaborone, Kanye and Molepolole.

▶▶ The **Batawana**, who broke away from the Bangwato, settled further north around the southern edges of the Okavango.

▶▶ The **Babirwa** come from the Tuli Block.

▶▶ The **Batswapong** come from the eastern regions around Selebi Phikwe.

▶▶ The **Bakgalagadi**, who are one of the oldest groups, live in the central regions of the Kalahari around Ghanzi and Kang.

The major non-Setswana speaking groups:

▶▶ The **Bakalanga**, largest group in the country, live around Francistown.

▶▶ The **Basarwa**, who were the earliest inhabitants of Botswana, live throughout the Central Kalahari and in the west.

▶▶ The **Banoka**, who are often referred to as the River Bushmen, traditionally were those who lived in the Okavango Delta. There are few true Banoka surviving today.

▶▶ The **Baherero**, who came from Namibia, have settled in towns such as Sehitwa and Toteng, along the western edges of the Okavango Delta, and in Maun.

▶▶ The **Bayei** live along the Panhandle in the northern regions of the Okavango Delta.

▶▶ The **Mbukushu** live along the Panhandle and in the villages of Etsha 6 and Etsha 13.

▶▶ The **Basubiya** live in the north-east in Kasane and along the Chobe River.

▶▶ **Europeans and Asians**, who began arriving in the early 19th century, have settled mostly in the urban areas and the Okavango Delta. The Ghanzi district was settled by a group of Afrikaans-speakers from South Africa.

BELOW LEFT: Intshupeleng Letsatsi is from Etsha 13.
BELOW MIDDLE: Because of their high protein and fat content, reproductive termites are a sought-after food source in the rural areas. They leave their mounds after the first rains and are collected with the aid of lanterns and candles, which attract the insects in their thousands.
BELOW RIGHT: Person Mothanka, who lives in the village of Nxamaseri, on his wedding day.

Strong-willed and resourceful, the people of Botswana are the backbone of their country.

More modern

Village life and the *kgotla*
In the past, with the exception of the semi-nomadic Bushmen, most other groups lived pastoral lifestyles in permanent settlements. Traditionally, these villages were located (for defensive reasons) in hilly regions, or around reliable water sources where grazing conditions were best. Homesteads, which consisted of circular huts, built with reeds or mud, had grass roofs and were usually surrounded by a pole or reed fence. Communal eating places and smaller huts built for storage purposes were situated in the centre of the village. Every family was entitled to land, where agricultural fields were planted, and a cattle post for keeping livestock. The village heads or chiefs (*kgosi*) were responsible for looking after the affairs of the community.

Maize porridge (papa to the locals) and boiled fish are the staple foods in and around the Okavango Delta.

The *kgotla*, or traditional meeting place, was the most significant spot within any village. Recognised by all as a place of respect, it was always to be found in the middle of the village or under the largest tree. This is where all social, judicial and political affairs of the community were discussed and dealt with.

Today, while most of the homesteads in the rural villages are built using modern fabricated materials of some sort, the *kgotla* and cattle posts remain integral to the stability of these communities.

Cattle
Cattle, and to a lesser extent goats and sheep, have always played an important social and economic role within Batswana society. Animal husbandry was central to the survival and success of most groups, other than the Basarwa and Bayei. Cattle in particular were kept, not only for food and clothing, but also as a measure of wealth. The larger their herd's size the greater the influence an individual or family had within the community. Cattle were also traditionally used as the primary means of exchange. Disputes and punishments handed down by the *kgotla* were settled with payments of cattle, and men paying their *bogadi* (bride price) would deliver cattle to the woman's family. Cattle still retain a prominent place in rural Botswana, and for many the herd remains the preferred store of wealth.

Totems
The occurrence of totems is common throughout Africa, and indeed the world. While some groups have non-animal totems, most within Botswana have animals as their group or community totem. The totem serves as a symbolic representation of a strong association with a specific animal, and with the natural world in general. The totem is given extraordinary respect, usually because of a specific event that has occurred in a group's history, or more generally because of the nature of the interaction between the group and their particular totem animal. The **Basubiya** live along the waterways of the Chobe River, which has always had a large population of hippopotamus, and so this species is their totem. For the **Bakwena** it is the crocodile, and for the **Batawana** the lion. Two more interesting associations concern the **Bangwato** and a community of Banoka, known as the **Xaniqwee**. The Bangwato totem is the duiker, a small nondescript antelope species, which is revered in their mythology for saving the life of a chief. The aardvark serves as the Xaniqwee totem, because when the group first trekked up to the Okavango region hundreds of years ago they had to cross the parched lands of the Kalahari. It was the aardvark that provided them with food, and more importantly with water that was found trapped in the animals' burrows. Out of respect, there are very specific restrictions on hunting or handling the totem animal.

On an overland or self-drive safari you'll pass this small general store on your way through the Khwai community between the Moremi Game Reserve and Savuti Marsh.

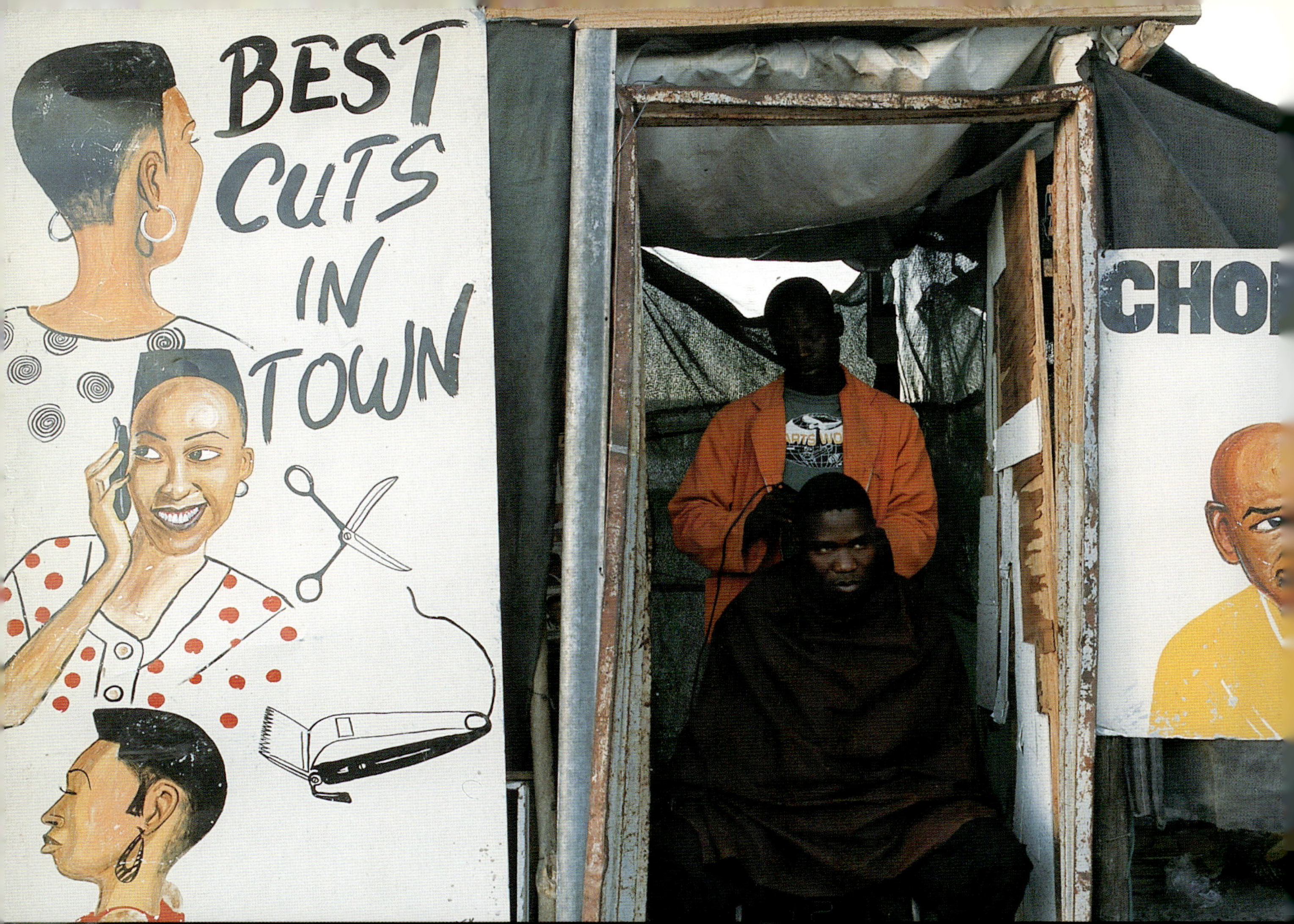
BEST
CUTS
IN
TOWN
CHO

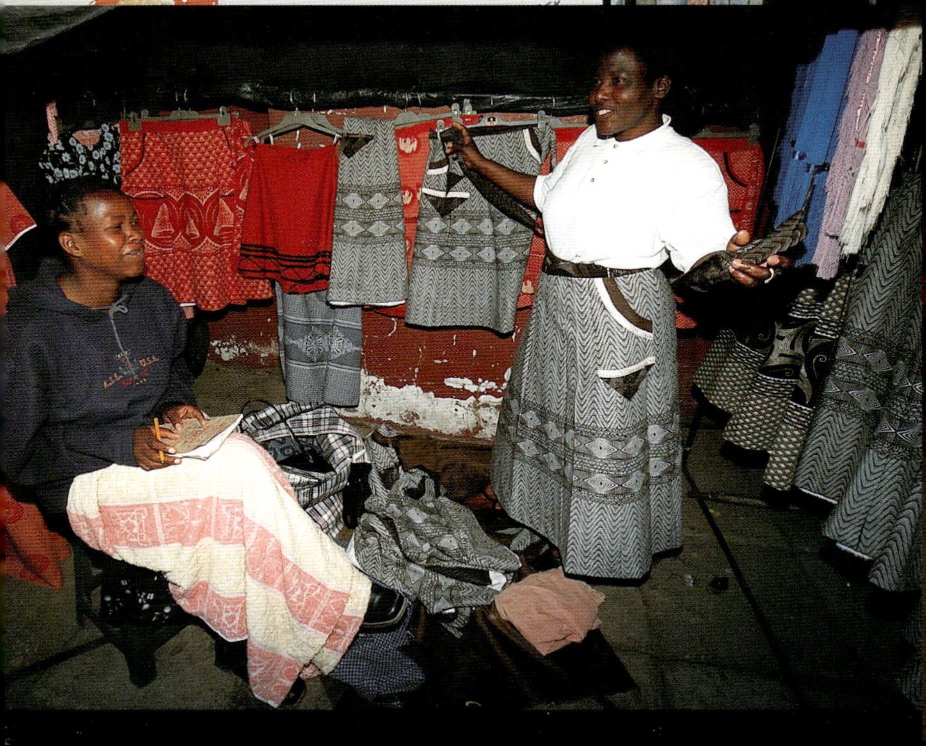

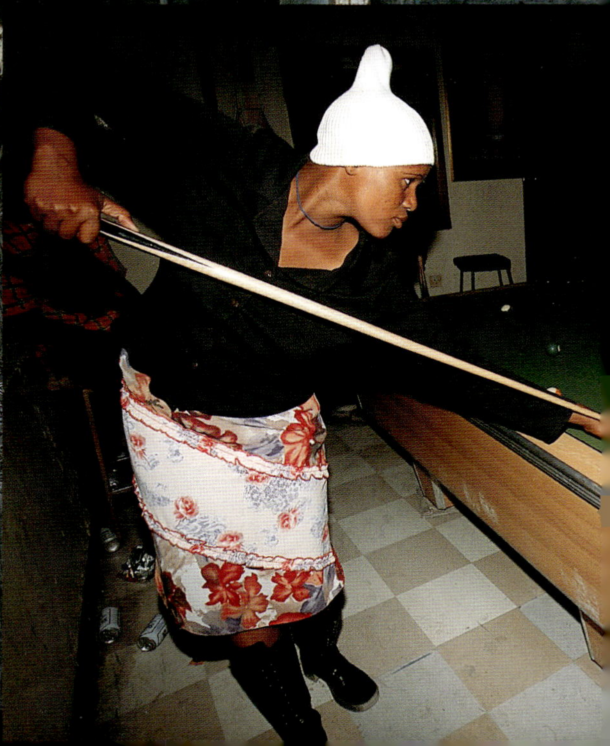

A selection of images from around the country, depicting the more modern aspects of a recently urbanised society.

A culture of ceremony

Religious beliefs

The Batswana are an extremely spiritual society and religion plays a leading role in their daily lives. Before the arrival of the colonial missionaries, the people worshipped **Modimo**, a greater God or Supreme Being who was also representative of the ancestors. They believed that a supernatural being was responsible for the creation of both humankind and the other animals and plants. For this reason, their cosmology reflects a strong connection between people and the natural environment.

For those that still follow a traditional belief system, **ancestral worship** is central to their daily religious practice, as it is believed that, if appeased, the ancestors will protect the family, strengthen the community and keep away ill omens. Ancestors are also invoked to promote auspicious seasonal events, such as the well-timed onset of the rains and a good-quality harvest. The **traditional healer** always plays a strong role in these belief systems, as the ancestral spirits are often contacted through them. The family head may also be the medium for contact.

In the early 1800s, the **London Missionary Society** became the first group to start operating in Botswana. They established the first educational institutions and, with these, the Christian word began to spread. This was the beginning of the disintegration of many traditional practices and beliefs. Today, approximately 30 percent of Batswana belong to one of the Christian churches (most are Catholic or Anglican), while over 65 percent adhere to the practices of the African Religion or still follow traditional beliefs. The African Religion comprises a variety of churches: the **Healing Church of Botswana**, the **Zionist Christian Church** and the **Apostolic Faith Mission**, for example, and these belong to two main movements: the **African Independent and Pentecostal churches**. These are indigenous religions that practise an integrated form of worship, combining the Christian liturgy with the more ritualistic elements of traditional ancestral worship. Very popular in the rural areas, the African Religion has a strong sense of community worship, rather than the more individualistic routine of modern Christianity.

Marriage

Traditionally, the Batswana were polygynous, with marriages mostly pre-arranged and taking place shortly after men and women complete their initiation rites into adulthood. Today, with the exception of the Baherero, most Batswana choose their own partners and the marriage ceremony has become an expression of the more contemporary nature of society. The arrangements are the responsibility of the groom's uncle, rather than the parents, and are negotiated over the course of a number of meetings between the respective families. The traditional custom of the groom paying a *bogadi* to the bride's family still exists amongst rural families. The price differs between groups, but it is often seven cows – one for each day of the week – or it may consist of a combination of cows, other livestock and money. Festivities usually take place over three days and, in the rural communities, everyone is entitled to attend. Each family will prepare a feast where livestock are slaughtered, providing food for the respective family members and friends. Once the groom and his uncle have delivered the bride price, then the ceremony may take place, after which there will be plenty of song and dance.

The different groups have different lines of inheritance, with some (the Mbukushu and certain groups within the Baherero, for example) being matrilineal. In a polygynous marriage, the children born to a man's head wife inherit the family estate.

Church elders from the Apostolic Faith Mission lead the congregation in prayer.

TOP: Song and dance are integral to the Sunday services conducted by the Healing Church of Botswana.
ABOVE: When the annual flood waters reach Maun, the various denominations from the African Religion take to the river to carry out baptisms.
FAR LEFT: In Bayei funeral ceremonies, the uncle of the deceased stands above the coffin while friends and family file past paying their last respects.
RIGHT: Tiny Sebadietla, from the village of Etsha 13, on her wedding day.

Collecting water using the donkey cart is a weekly chore, and is often the responsibility of the children in rural families.

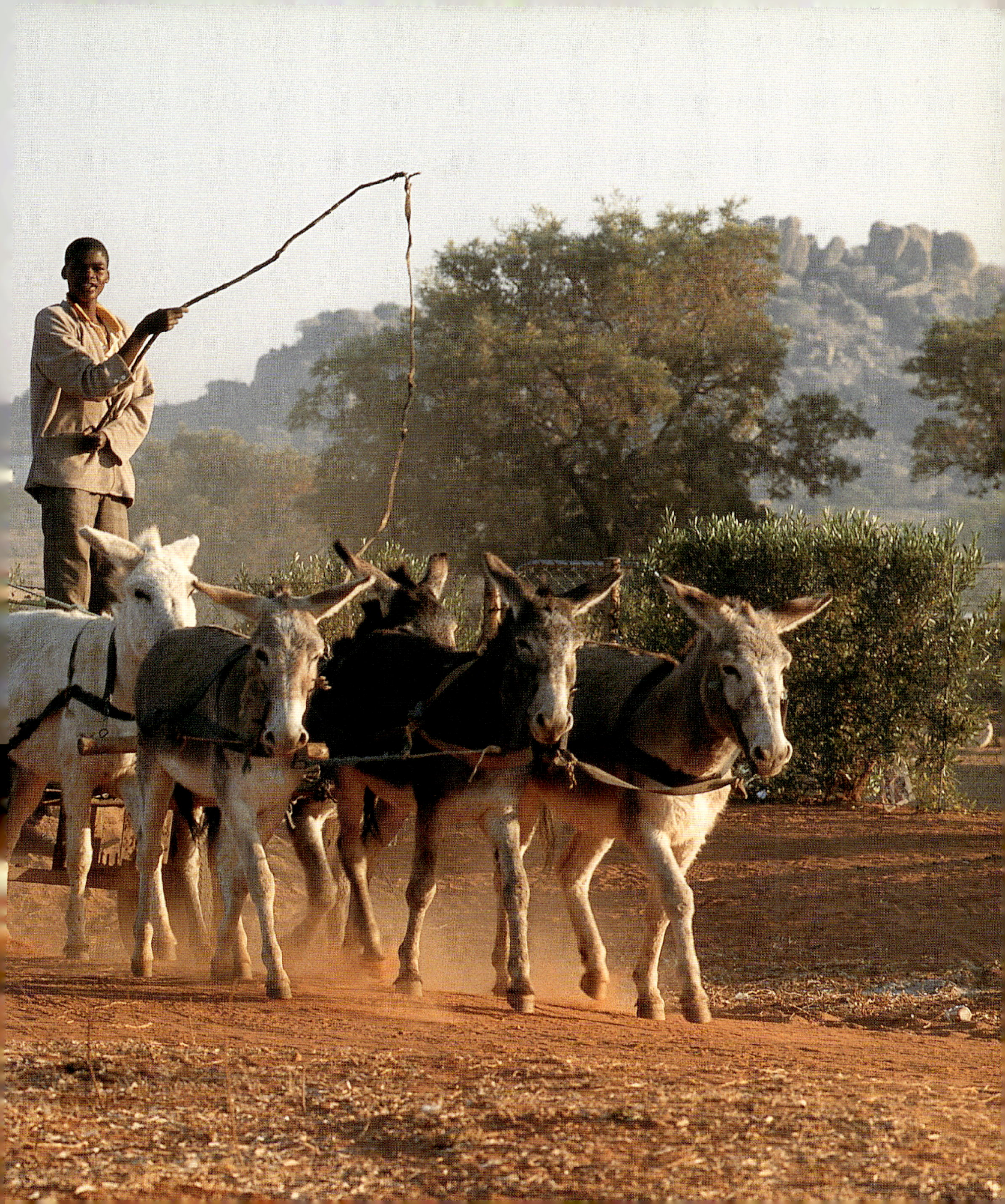

So to speak

While **English** is the official language and **Setswana** the national language, there are over 20 other languages spoken in the country, which are mostly used by the non-Setswana-speaking groups. **Sekalanga**, spoken by the Bakalanga, is the most commonly used of these languages. Almost 90 percent of citizens speak Setswana as their mother tongue and, although English is spoken throughout the urban areas and within all tourist facilities, you may have to try a little harder to be understood in the rural areas. Below are some words and phrases to help.

Pula

The word '*pula*', which appears on the national coat of arms, is a significant one for the people of Botswana, as it embraces many meanings. In its literal sense it means '**let there be rain**' – in a country that is mostly semi-arid, rainfall is precious and appreciated as a blessed event. Hence '*pula*' is also the name given to the local currency, with one Pula consisting of 100 thebe. Pula is also the country's motto and rallying cry (in this context it means 'shield'), and is shouted out by crowds at football matches whenever the national team, 'The Zebras', scores a goal. Those attending traditional village gatherings (*kgotla*) or political rallies may respond with cries of '*pula*' as a way of enthusiastically supporting the speaker.

When greeting a man/woman – *Dumêla rra/mma*

When greeting a group of people – *Dumêlang*

How are you? – *O tsogile jang, Le kae* or *Wareng?* (informal)

I am fine – *Ke tsogile sentle* or *Ke teng* (informal)

Yes – *Ee*

No – *Nnyaa*

Help! – *Nthusa!*

I am lost – *Ke la tlhegile*

Today – *Gompieno*

Tomorrow – *Kamoso*

Yesterday – *Maabane*

Everything is fine / no problems – *Go siame*

Please – *Tsweetswee*

What is the price? – *K bokae?*

What is your name? – *Leina la gago ke mang?*

Where do you come from? – *O tswa kae?*

I come from South Africa – *Ke tswa kwa Afrika Borwa*

Cheers – *Pula* or *Sharpu* (slang)

Thank you – *Ke itumetse* or *Kea leboga*

Is Air Botswana always half a day late? – *A sefofane sa Botswana senna sele kwa mouago metsotso e kannang thatsaro mo letsatsing?*

Why is there a hyena in my tent? – *Ke eng phiri e le mo tante yame?*

Do we eat so much at every camp? – *A re a kgora janna nako tshotlhe mo campend?*

Can you show me the quickest way out of Maun? – *Ntshopotse tsela e bofefo ya go tswa mo Maun?*

Goodbye/stay well (if you are leaving) – *Sala sentle*

Goodbye/go well (to person leaving) – *Tsamaya sentle*

OPPOSITE LEFT: While drug use is not a major problem, the country does battle with one of the highest HIV/AIDS infection rates in the world.
OPPOSITE RIGHT: The typical style depicted in so much of the artwork painted by Bushman artists.

ABOVE LEFT: A classroom mural at a community school in D'Kar.
ABOVE RIGHT: A list of offences from the Gweta Police Station. Botswana on the whole enjoys a low crime rate.

myth & MYSTERY

Traditional dancing is usually done to the accompaniment of drumming by the men and clapping by the women. Dry seedpods or moth cocoons are worn as rattles, tied to the legs of dancers.

The Bayei and Mbukushu people live along the Panhandle in the northern regions of the Okavango. While the Bayei use *mekoro* to get about the river system in search of fish, the Mbukushu have a more agriculture-based lifestyle along the banks of the river. For both, it is a life closely associated with the Delta's waterways and its creatures, one of which is the ever-present crocodile.

Boboko Jwa Kwena

Both the Bayei and Mbukushu believe in the powers of the **traditional healer** and the **spirit medium**. The *ngaka* (sometimes also known as a *sangoma*) has a very significant position within any community, and is trusted with all things related to individual and group well-being. They are continually consulted on issues of health, family, the future and the natural world. The darker side of life however is represented by the *moloi*, a witch or wizard, who is only ever linked with bad omens and evil deeds. A belief in witches and wizards is common throughout rural Africa, as they provide answers to mysterious calamities that befall families and communities. For those who believe, everything about the *moloi* is disturbing — they operate at night, usually coming from within the community, and their identities remain unknown. It is thought that in the dark of the night they are able to become two people, with the physical body remaining asleep while the spirit body leaves to carry out sinister acts. The most potent **muti** (medicine or potion) available to the *moloi* is *boboko jwa kwena*, the 'brain of the crocodile'.

Believers say that when *boboko jwa kwena* is used against someone, it brings disease, physical disability or material loss, but most often death.

In the Okavango, a *moloi* is unlikely to kill a crocodile in order to get hold of its brain, as that would arouse suspicion. It is preferable to seek out a dead animal. Once the brain has been removed, it is dried and ground into powder form and then stored in a small container, either underground or in a dark place. **Hyenas and owls** have a strong mythological connection with the *moloi*, born out of the nocturnal habits and haunting calls of both animals; it is believed that they deliver the *moloi* to their chosen victims. Administering the *muti* is done by placing it in the food or drink of the victim, or by dropping it into the open mouth of a sleeping person. The potion works slowly, but once the victim begins deteriorating they are likely to die. Once dead the body quickly turns a green colour — a confirmation that crocodile brain has been used. That is why, if dead crocodiles are ever found by anyone other than a *moloi*, they are always burnt.

The brain of the crocodile is the most powerful *muti* available to those who practise witchcraft. Anyone other than the *moloi* who finds a dead crocodile will ensure the animal is burnt to ash, so that its brain cannot be used.

The stars above

The belief system of the Bushmen, more than any other, embodies a spiritual connection to nature. Their mythology is rich with symbolic accounts of events and facts that would be otherwise inexplicable. Spending every night out under the crisp clear skies of the Kalahari, they naturally looked up at the heavenly spectacle above them and wondered how the stars came to fill the night skies.

Traditionally, the Bushmen were hunter-gatherers who lived mostly in small communities consisting of extended family members. So, when any young maiden began her first menstrual cycle, it was a time of great celebration as she was now becoming a woman, who would soon bear children – and children represented the future of the family and the general well-being of the greater community. On the day her cycle began, the young woman would move with her mother to a specially prepared hut, where they would stay for the duration of her menstruation. Her mother would use this opportunity to discuss her approaching womanhood and issues of marriage and childbirth. In the meantime, the men would go out and hunt, in preparation for the feast that was held on the last day.

Once her period of menstruation was over, the young woman and her mother would emerge from the hut to join the rest of the community in a final celebration. That night, a bonfire would be lit, and everyone would feast on the meat brought in by the hunters. After everyone had eaten well, singing and dancing would carry on through the night and well into the early hours of the morning. Just before the first light appeared, when the bonfire had been reduced to glowing embers, the young woman would kneel at the fire and, with her hands together, collect up a heap of low-burning coals. She would then stand looking up into the skies and, with everyone gathered around, she would fling the ashes high into the sky. For the Bushman people the stars represent all the young maidens who have passed into womanhood.

BELOW: Young women from the Gudikwa Bushman community with an array of adornments made from ostrich shell, seed pods and leather.
RIGHT: An elderly woman from the Tsodilo Hills Bushman community.

travel DIRECTORY

Travel advisory

LOCAL TIME
GMT (Greenwich Mean Time) plus two hours.

WEATHER
Because most of the country lies within the tropics some authors refer to the climate as being tropical, but it would be more accurate to call it continental semi-arid. Rainfall is generally low and unreliable, and drought conditions are not uncommon. The summer season – from October to March – is usually hot and reasonably wet, while the winter is mild and dry. Average rainfall patterns vary a great deal. The highest rainfall is recorded in the far north-east, along the Chobe River, where it averages over 650 mm per annum. The lowest is in the central and south-western regions, where the average is below 250 mm. About 80 percent of rainfall occurs during the months from December through to February. The average temperatures are 26° Celsius in the summer months (with highs of over 40°) and 15° in the winter (the lows sometimes reach below 8°, but seldom approach freezing point).

WHEN TO TRAVEL
Because of the mild climate, Botswana is pleasant throughout the year. However, here is a guideline for those visiting with specific activities in mind: While the best wildlife viewing generally occurs during the drier months, from May through to early November, summer still offers a great safari experience as this is when most of the plains game species drop their calves.

For bird watching, September through to early March, is the most rewarding time in terms of the number of species and density of birds you'll encounter. For the fishing folk, the best time for catching bream is from April through to August, and tiger fishing peaks from August to early December. Because the flood levels are at their highest during winter, this is the best time for a full *mokoro* safari. If you're doing a self-drive route, check on local road conditions during the summer months as heavy rainfalls often render the dirt roads in the wildlife areas unusable.

HEALTH AND MEDICINE
Botswana is classified as a medium- to high-risk malaria area. All travellers should consult their local medical practitioner for advice on what malaria prophylaxis to take prior to departure. No inoculations are required, unless you are arriving from a yellow fever region. Beware of swimming in stagnant water, as there is the possibility of contracting bilharzia. While all tap water in the country is safe for human consumption, most hotels, lodges and camps provide bottled drinking water. Most safari lodges and camps have comprehensive medical aid kits on their premises.

EMERGENCY SERVICE NUMBERS
Ambulance – 997
Fire – 998
Police – 999
Medrescue – 911
The National Telephone Operator – 100
Lifeline Botswana – 391 1290
Women Against Rape – 686 0865
MRI Botswana (Medrescue evacuations) – 390 1601
Automobile Association Botswana – 395 9444
Avenue Medical Centre, Gaborone – 390 7771
Pana Medical Consultation Clinic, Francistown – 241 8666
Delta Medical Centre, Maun – 686 2999
Chobe Private Clinic, Kasane – 625 1555
Life Care Clinic, Ghanzi – 659 6375
Medi Clinical Centre, Serowe – 463 0378

PUBLIC HOLIDAYS
1 January – New Year's Day
2 January – Public Holiday
March or April – Easter weekend (Good Friday and Easter Saturday, Sunday and Monday)
April or May – Ascension Day
1 May – Labour Day
1 July – Sir Seretse Khama Day
14 July – President's Day
30 September – Botswana Day (Independence Day)
1 October – Public Holiday
25 December – Christmas Day
26 December – Boxing Day

VISAS AND BORDER POSTS

Entering and leaving the country is usually a formality, and travellers are unlikely to experience any hassles from officials, provided that you comply with all relevant laws and you behave with due respect. For visa requirements, check with your nearest travel agent before departing, as certain countries do require visas. Generally, citizens of European Union countries, Scandinavia, USA and South Africa do not require visas. Travellers from these countries will most often be issued with a 30-day visa, which can be extended to a maximum of 90 days. For travellers arriving by air, Gaborone, Maun and Kasane are the regular flight entry points. No European or North American airline flies directly into Gaborone. For road travellers the country is accessible by tarred road from all neighbouring countries. The following are the main border posts (note that opening and closing times change so these should be treated as guidelines):

FROM NAMIBIA
Mamuno/Buitepos: 7 am to midnight
Ngoma Bridge: 7 am to 6 pm
Mohembo: 6 am to 6 pm

FROM SOUTH AFRICA
Tlokweng (Gaborone): 6 am to 10 pm
Martins Drift (Limpopo River): 8 am to 6 pm
All other border posts on the Limpopo River: 8 am to 4 pm
Pioneer Gate (Lobatse): 6 am to 10 pm
All border posts on the Molopo River: 8 am to 4 pm

FROM ZAMBIA
Kazangula Ferry: 6 am to 6 pm

FROM ZIMBABWE
Kasane: 6 am to 6 pm
Pandamatenga: 7.30 am to 4 pm
Ramokgwebana (Plumtree): 6 am to 8 pm

SAFETY AND SECURITY

Botswana is one of the safest countries, if not the safest country, to travel in Africa. It has an unsurpassed record when it comes to the safety of its tourists. While serious crime is almost non-existent, petty theft may occur in the cities and major towns. Road travellers will encounter police and veterinary road-blocks through most of the country, so carry your travel documents and driver's licence (South African and International driver's licences are valid in Botswana for six months) at all times. For those carrying firearms and meat products, make sure you have the necessary paperwork on you.

CURRENCY AND BANKING

The local unit of currency is the Pula, which is divided into 100 Thebe. The following notes are in circulation: P100, P50, P20 and P10. For international travellers the recommended form of payment is by credit card, and all the major ones are accepted at most tourist facilities and in retail outlets in the cities and larger towns. US dollars and Euros are the recommended currencies for those bringing cash. South African Rands are accepted in most major towns and in all tourist facilities. There are five major banks and a number of exchange bureaux operating in the country. While most have branches in the cities and larger towns, do not expect to find any banking facilities in the rural areas and in the smaller towns. There are no major currency controls.

FEES FOR PARKS AND RESERVES

These rates were applicable to all parks and reserves, other than Kgalagadi Transfrontier Park and Mbuasehube, at the time of going to press. Fees may have been adjusted since then, so treat these as a guideline. To avoid disappointment, make sure you book your campsite with the Department of Wildlife and National Parks before departing on safari. Payments are made only at the entrance gates and must be in Pula, US Dollars, Euros, UK Pounds or South African Rands.

PARK ENTRY FEES PER DAY
(CITIZEN / RESIDENT / NON-RESIDENT)
Adults, 18 years and above: P10 / P30 / P120
Children, 8 to 17 inclusive: P5 / P15 / P60
Children, under 8: Free / Free / Free

CAMPING FEES PER NIGHT
(CITIZEN / RESIDENT / NON-RESIDENT)
Adults, 18 years and above: P5 / P20 / P30
Children, 8 to 17 inclusive: P2.50 / P10 / P15
Children, under 8: Free / Free / Free

VEHICLE FEES
BOTSWANA REGISTERED / FOREIGN REGISTERED
Motor vehicles under 3 500 kilograms:
P10 / P50
Motor vehicles 3 500–7 000 kilograms:
P500 / P1 000
Motor vehicles over 7 000 kilograms:
P800 / P1 500

TRAVEL TIPS
▶▶ If you're on a self-drive trip and are using a borrowed vehicle, make sure that you are in possession of a certified letter from the owner detailing permission for you to drive the vehicle.

▶▶ For those who are travelling by road: adhere to the speed limits, as Botswana does use trapping equipment.

▶▶ Try to avoid travelling on open national roads after dark, as domestic stock can be an extreme hazard.

▶▶ Do not, under any circumstances, resort to bribing officials. The country has a low tolerance for bribery and corruption, and you may end up in prison. To report instances of attempted bribery and corruption, telephone this number: +267-391-4002 or toll free: 0800-700-100, or email: reporttodced@gov.bw

▶▶ Air Botswana is notoriously bad with their booking system. Hustle and double-check before accepting no for an answer.

▶▶ In general, retail outlets carry a sufficient variety of goods and almost everything you'll need can be purchased in the cities and major towns. Fuel is also readily available throughout the country, although in the central and south-western regions the distances between fuel stations can be great.

▶▶ Do not venture near any facility that belongs to the Botswana Defence Force, and refrain from photographing anyone in uniform.

▶▶ The air charter companies that fly into the Okavango Delta and other safari destinations have strict 12 kilogram per person baggage limits. These must be adhered to.

▶▶ Contrary to what a lot of the reading material on Botswana says, December and January can be very cool months because of rainfall. If travelling during these months, carry a set of warm clothes as well.

WANT TO KNOW MORE?
The following books are recommended:

The Miracle Rivers, Peter and Beverly Pickford (Southern)
Hunting with the Moon, Dereck and Beverly Joubert (National Geographic Society)
Okavango: Jewel of the Kalahari, Karen Ross (Struik)
Okavango: Africa's Wetland Wilderness, Adrian Bailey (Struik)
This is Botswana, Daryl and Sharna Balfour (New Holland)
Elephants for Africa, Randall Jay Moore
The Lost World of the Kalahari, Sir Laurens van der Post (Penguin)
Kalahari: Life's Variety in Dune and Delta, Michael Main (Southern)
Cry of the Kalahari, Mark and Delia Owens (Fontana/Collins)
Botswana: A Brush with the Wild, Paul Augustinus (Struik)
A Marriage of Inconvenience: The Persecution of Seretse and Ruth Khama, Michael Dutfield (Unwin Hyman)
History of Botswana, T Tlou and A Campbell (Macmillan Botswana)

TOURISM REPRESENTATIVES

Ministry of Environment, Wildlife and Tourism: Private Bag 0047, Gaborone, tel: +267-395-3024, email: botswanatourism@gov.bw, www.discoverbotswana.com or www.botswanatourism.org

Maun Tourism Office: PO Box 439, Maun, tel: +267-686-0492, email: tourism.maun@gov.bw

Kasane Tourism Office: PO Box 66, Kasane, tel: +267-625-0357, email: tourism.kasane@gov.bw

Francistown Tourism Office: Private Bag F428, Francistown, tel: +267-241-8192, email: tourism.francistown@gov.bw

Hotel & Tourism Association of Botswana (HATAB): Private Bag 00423, Gaborone, tel: +267-395-7144, email: hatab@info.bw

Botswana Wildlife Management Association (BWMA): Private Bag 098, Maun, tel: +267-686-2671, email: trophy@info.bw

Air Botswana: PO Box 92, Gaborone, tel: +267-395-2812/397-4361, email: commercial@airbotswana.co.bw

INTERNATIONAL TOURISM REPRESENTATIVES

USA: Kartagener Associates Inc.: 631 Commack Road, Suite 1A, Commack, NY 11725, USA, tel: +1-631-858-1252 or toll free: +1-877-268-7926, email: botswanatourism@kainyc.com

UK: Southern Skies Marketing: Index House, St George's Lane, Ascot, Berkshire SL5 7EU, United Kingdom, tel: +44-1344-636-430, email: botswanatourism@southern-skies.co.uk

GERMANY: Interface International GmbH: Petersburger Strasse 94, 10247, Berlin, Germany, tel: +49-30-420-88012, email: botswanarep@t-online.de

DEPARTMENT OF WILDLIFE AND NATIONAL PARKS

Parks and Reserves Reservations, Gaborone Office: PO Box 131, Gaborone, tel: +267-318-0774, fax: +267-318-0775

Parks and Reserves Reservations, Maun Office: PO Box 20364, Maun, tel: +267-686-1265, fax: +267-686-0053

SAFARI OPERATORS

Okavango Wilderness Safaris: Private Bag 14, Maun, tel: +267-686-0086, email: enquiry@wilderness.co.za
Reservations: tel: +27-11-807-1800, email: enquiry@wilderness.co.za, www.wilderness-safaris.com

Sanctuary Lodges: Private Bag 45, Maun, tel: +267-686-2688, email: osouchon@sanctuarylodges.com
Reservations: tel: +27-11-781-1497, email: southernafrica@sanctuarylodges.com, www.sanctuarylodges.com

Desert and Delta Safaris: PO Box 310, Maun, tel: +267-686-1243, email: ddsres@botsnet.bw
Reservations: tel: +27-11-706-0861, email: reservations@desertdelta.com, www.desertdelta.com

Kwando Safaris: PO Box 550, Maun, tel: +267-686-1449, email: reservations@kwando.co.za, www.kwando.co.za

Orient Express Safaris: PO Box 100, Maun, tel: +267-686-0302, email: gtb.mngr.@info.bw
Reservations: tel: +27-11-481-6052, email: reservations@orient-express-safaris.co.za, www.orient-express-safaris.com

Mashatu Game Reserve: PO Box 26, Lentswe Le Moriti, tel: +267-264-5321, email: mashatu@info.bw
Reservations: tel: +27-31-765-2900, email: reservations@malamala.com, www.mashatu.com

Linyanti Explorations: PO Box 22, Kasane, tel: +267-625-0505, email: info@linyanti.com, www.linyanti.com

Uncharted Africa Safari Company: PO Box 173, Francistown, tel: +267-241-2277, email: ucchartered@info.bw, www.uncharteredafrica.com

Okavango Tours and Safaris: PO Box 39, Maun, tel: +267-686-0220, email: okavangotours@okavango.bw

The Booking Company: Private Bag 0198, Maun, tel: +267-686-0022, email: book@info.bw

Go Wild Safaris: PO Box 056, Kasane, tel: +267-625-0259/1297, email: go.wild@info.bw

Ker & Downey: PO Box 27, Maun, tel: +267-686-0376, email: safari@kerdowney.bw, www.kerdowney.com

Chobe Travel Shop: Private Bag K39, Kasane, tel: +267-625-1754, email: travel@botsnet.bw

NATURE RESERVES
Mokolodi Nature Reserve (includes chalets, restaurant and campsite): PO Box 170, Gaborone, tel: +267-596-1955/6, email: mokolodi@info.bw
Khama Rhino Sanctuary (includes chalets and campsite): PO Box 10, Serowe, tel: +267-463-0713, email: krst@botsnet.bw

ADVENTURE SAFARIS
Okavango Horse Safaris: Private Bag 23, Maun, tel: +267-686-1671, email: ohsnx@info.bw
African Horse Back Safaris: PO Box 20538, Maun, tel: +267-686-1523, email: sjhorses@info.bw
Limpopo Valley Horse Safaris: PO Box 26, Lentswe Le Moriti, tel: +267-264-5321, email lvhs@infotech.co.za
Elephant Back Safaris: Private Bag 332, Maun, tel: +267-686-1260, email: ebs@info.bw

MOBILE SAFARIS
Afro Ventures: PO Box 323 Kasane, tel: +267-625-0119, email: jnb@afroventures.com
Capricorn Safaris: Private Bag 021, Maun, tel: +267-686-1165, email: capsaf@info.bw
Crocodile Camp Safaris: PO Box 46, Maun, tel: +267-686-0796, email: sales@botswana.com
Drifters Adventure Tours: Private Bag 205, Maun, tel: +267-713-04472, email: mauncamp@hotmail.com
Drumbeat Safaris: PO Box, 20228, Maun, tel: +267-686-3096, email: drumbeat@info.bw
Eco Africa Botswana: Private Bag BO 372, Maun, tel: +267-686-2427, email: rogersafaris@dynabyte.bw
Game Trails: Private Bag BO13, Maun, tel: +267-686-0369, email: gametrails@botsnet.bw
Gavin Blair Safaris: Private Bag K19, Kasane, tel: +267-625-0237, email: gbs@gavinblairsafaris.com
Kalahari Kavango Safari Company: Private Bag 053, Maun, tel: +267-686-0981, email: kksafari@dynabyte.bw
Karibu Safaris: Private Bag 39, Maun, tel: +267-686-1225, email: karibu@karibu.co.za
Kgori Safaris: Private Bag 146, Maun, tel: +267-686-5788, email: kgorisaf@info.bw
Masson Safaris: Private Bag 257, Maun, tel: +267-686-2442, email: massonsafaris@botsnet.bw
Maun Rest Camp Safaris: PO Box 250, Maun, tel: +267-686-3472, email: simonjoyce@info.bw
Okavango Polers Trust: PO Box 24, Seronga, tel: +267-687-6861, email: sue@okavango.co.bw
Papadi Safaris and Tours: Private Bag 114, Maun, tel: +267-716-20855, email: papadi@info.bw
Penduka Safaris: PO Box 66, Maun, tel: +267-686-4539, email: sitatunga@info.bw
Waterways: Private Bag 041, Maun, tel: +267-686-0364, email: nm@info.bw
Wild Lifestyles: PO Box 66, Maun, tel: +267-686-3664, email: mikepenman@info.bw
Wilderness Dawning: Private Bag BO 17, Maun, tel: +267-686-4270, email: wd@info.bw

CULTURAL TOURS AND SAFARIS
Afrika Calls: PO Box 726, Maun, tel: +267-680-0710, email: afrikacalls@botsnet.bw
Cultural Tours Botswana: Private Bag 46, Maun, tel: +267-686-1823, email: jdavey@dynabyte.bw
Trail Blazers: PO Box 35, Ghanzi, tel: +267- 659-7525, email: trailblazers@botsnet.bw

CAMPS AND LODGES
Deception Valley Lodge: PO Box 818, Ghanzi, tel: +27-12-346-6864, email: res@deceptionvalley.co.za
Leroo-La-Tau: P.O. Box 38, Khumaga, tel: +267-686-8407, email: 2attract@bushmail.net
Maun Lodge: PO Box 376, Maun, tel:+267-686-3939, email: maun.lodge@info.bw
Meno A Kwena Tented Camp: Private Bag 053, Maun, tel: +267-686-0981, email: kksafari@dynabyte.bw
Modumo Lodge: PO Box 66, Maun, tel: +267-680-0880, email: reservations@modumo.com
Motsentsela Tree Lodge: PO Box 236, Maun, tel: +267-680-0757, email: treelodge@dynabyte.bw
Nxamaseri Lodge: Private Bage 159, Maun, tel: +267-687-8015/6, email: nxa.lodge@info.bw
The following establishments also offer camping:
Audi Camp: Private Bag 28, Maun, tel: +267-686-0599, email: audicamp@info.bw
Camp Itumela: Private Bag 45, Palapye, tel: +267-718-06771/715-09247

Chobe Safari Lodge: PO Box 10, Kasane, tel: +267-625-0336, email: reservations@chobelodge.co.bw
Drotsky's Cabins: PO Box 115, Shakawe, tel: +267-687-5035, email: drotskys@info.bw
Guma Lagoon Camp: Private Bag 23, Maun, tel: +267-687-4626, email: guma.property@info.bw
Kwa Nokeng Lodge: PO Box 10, Sherwood, tel: +267-491-5908, email: clinton@botsnet.bw
Maun Rest Camp: PO Box 250, Maun, tel: +267-686-3472, email: simonjoyce@info.bw
Nata Lodge: PO Box 10, Nata, tel: +267-621-1210, email: natalodge@info.bwIsland
Island Safari lodge: PO Box 116, Maun, tel: +267-686-0300, email: island@info.bw
Santawani Lodge: PO Box 21797, Maun, tel: +267-680-0664, email: santawani@dynabyte.bw
Sepopa Swamp Stop: PO Box 22028, Maun, tel: +267-687-7073, email: swampstop@info.bw

HUNTING OPERATORS
Blackbeard and Hepburn Safaris: PO Box 104, Kasane, tel: +267-625-1252, email: cbhsaf@botsnet.bw
Holbrow Hunting Safaris: Private Bag 332, Maun, tel: +267-686-1260, email: ebs@info.bw
Linyanti Explorations: PO Box 22, Kasane, tel: +267-625-0505, email: selinda@info.bw
Rann Safaris: PO Box 40, Maun, tel: +267-686-1821, email: rannsafaris@yahoo.com
Safaris Botswana: PO Box 20, Maun, tel: +267-686-3055, email: saf.bots@info.bw
Safari South: PO Box 40, Maun, tel: +267-686-1849, email: safarisouth@yahoo.com

AIR CHARTER COMPANIES
Delta Air: PO Box 39, Maun, tel: +267-686-1682, email: synergy@info.bw
Mack Air: Private Bag 329, Maun, tel: +267-686-0675, email: mack.air@info.bw
Moremi Air Services: Private Bag 187, Maun, tel: +267-686-2078, email: moremi.air@info.bw
Okavango Helicopters: Private Bag 174, Maun, tel: +267-686-5797, email: okavangoheli@dynabyte.bw
Sefofane: Private Bag 159, Maun, tel: +267-686-0778, email: sefofane@info.bw

HOTELS
Cresta Marakanelo Group: Private Bag 00272, Gaborone, tel: +267-391-2222, email: reservations@cresta.co.bw; www.cresta-hospitality.com
Gaborone Sun: Private Bag 0016, Gaborone, tel: +267-395-1111, email: gads-res@sunint.co.za
The Grand Palm Hotel: Private Bag BR 105, Gaborone, tel: +267-391-2999, email: info@grandpalm.bw
Kalahari Arms Hotel: PO Box 29, Ghanzi, tel: +267-659-6298, email: afikrainfo@postnet.co.za
Sedia Hotel: Private Bag 0058, Maun, tel: +267-686-0177, email: sedia@info.bw

GOLF COURSES
Phakalane Golf Estate and Hotel Resort: PO Box 132, Gaborone, tel: +267-393-6490, email for golf: rayers@phakalane.co.bw, email for resort: stjirokohe@phakalane.co.bw
Mowana Safari Lodge: PO Box 266, Kasane, tel: +267-625-0300, email: mowana@info.bw

CAR RENTAL
Avis: PO Box 790, Gaborone, tel: +267-397-5469, email: avisbots@botsnet.bw
Budget: Private Bag SK5, Gaborone, tel: +267-390-2030, email: botswana@budget.co.za
Imperial: PO Box 403282, Gaborone, tel: +267-390-6676, email: imperialfleetbots@it.bw

INVESTMENT OPPORTUNITIES
Botswana Export Development and Investment Authority (BEDIA): PO Box 3122, Gaborone, tel: +267-318-1931, email: bedia@bedia.bw; www.bedia.co.bw
Botswana Development Corporation: Private Bag 160, Gaborone, tel: +267-365-1378/00, email: enquiries@bdc.bw

Because of the terrain, small charter aircraft are used to move guests from lodge to lodge within the Okavango Delta.

Index

Numbers in *italics* indicate illustrations.

Accomodation 60, 64–5, 85, 187–8
Aha Hills 155
ancestral worship 172
Angola 30, 89, 98, 148
arts and crafts
    art shop *25*
    baskets 66, *157, 162, 163*
    Bushman art *159, 160, 176*
    Bushman crafts 82
    Bushman rock art 66, *74*, 107
    pottery *156–7*, 159

Baloi, BK *126*
Balozi Kingdom 30
Bechuanaland 32, 107
Bestelink, PJ 39, *126*
billboards *63, 65, 94, 170–1*
birds
    African skimmers 36, 97
    bateleur *133*
    black crake *132*
    black egret *130–1*
    carmine bee-eaters 49, 97, *133*
    fish eagle *132, 133*
    flamingo 77, 97, 105
    kites, yellow-billed 49
    ostrich *132*
    Pel's fishing owl 36, 97, *131*
    pelican 77, 105
    slaty egrets 36, 97
    wattled cranes 36, *95*, 97
    woodland kingfishers 49
    yellow-billed kites 49
bogadi 172, 189
Botswana country map 69
British South Africa Company 32, 107

Cape Colony 30, 32
carmine bee-eaters 49, *97, 133*
cattle industry 19, 30, 32, 33, 148, *149, 168*
Central Kalahari Game Reserve 94, 117, 154, *155*
Chibua, Isaac *158*, 159
chiefs
    Bathoen1: 32
    Khama111: 32
    Moremi111: 101, 107
    Mzilikazi 32
    Sebele 32
    Sechele 32
    Sekgoma 32
    Tshekedi 32
Chobe National Park 42, *73*, 94, 96, 97, 103, 117, 125, *142–3*
Chobe River 30, 36, 42, 49, 53, 76, 90, *102–103*, 117, *133–5, 144*, 168
Chobe, Savuti and Pans map 73
churches *172, 173*

communications
    cellphones *12*, 14
    internet 60, 78
    phone shop *24–5*
    radio mast *16*
    satellite dish 14, *15*
    telephone booths *14*
    telephone lines 78
concessions
    Chitabe 96
    Jao 36, *108*, 125
    Kwando 42, 96, 97, 124
    Linyati 27, 96, 97, 124
    Sandibi 96
    Selinda 96, 97
    Vumbura *37*, 96, 97, 121
conservation 150

D'Kar 55, 64, 65, *159*, 177
dancing display *161, 178–9*
Department of Tourism 26
diamond mines *21*
diamonds 11, 19, 20, 22, 33
Difaqane 32, 189
donkeys 14, 65, 85, *174–5*

Eco-tourism 11, 20, 26, 27, 33
eco-tourism sites (see Parks, Major)
    Abu Camp 36, *40, 41, 120*, 125
    Camp Itulema 62
    Central Kalahari Game Reserve 94, 117, 154, *155*
    Chief's Island 36, 97, 101, *109*
    Chobe Chilwero 42, *113*
    Chobe National Park 42, *73*, 94, 96, 97, 103, 117, 125, *142–3*
    Chobe Safari Lodge 42, *112*
    Drotsky's Cabins 36
    Gemsbok National Park 42, 154
    Gudikwa village *27*
    Guma Lagoon Camp 36
    Jack's Camp *43, 110–111*, 126
    Jao Camp 36, *108*
    Kalahari 32, 42, 55, 62, 66, 89, 90, 124, 181
    Kebala Camp 125
    Kgalagadi Transfrontier Park 42, 94, 97, 154
    Khutse Game Reserve 94, 154
    King's Pool *27, 115*
    Kubu Island 42
    Kujwana 36, *126*
    Mabuasehube Game Reserve 94, 154
    Macatoo 36
    Makgadikgadi Pans *27, 43, 44, 51, 77, 90, 104, 105, 115*, 117, 126
    Mashatu Game Reserve 42, *45, 107, 121*
    Meno a Kwena Camp 155
    Mokolodi Nature Reserve 42, *43*

Mombo Camp 36, 97, *109, 116*, 124
Moremi Game Park 42, *72*, 94, 96, 97, 101, 103, 117, 118, *119*
Nata Lodge 62
Nata Sanctuary 77
Nxai Pan 94, 96, 105
Nxamaseri Lodge 36, *114*
Oddballs 36, *121*
Okavango Delta 30, 36, *37*, 56, 62, 86–7, 90, 91, 93, 95, 96, 97, 98, 99, *100–101, 114*, 124, 126, 133, 143, 148
Panhandle 36, 51, 53, 66, 67, 74, 97, 98, *114–115*, 117, 121, 131, 179
Planet Baobab 42, *76, 110–111*
Savuti Bush Camp 42, *112*, 117
Savuti Channel *92–3*, 96, 97, 103
Savuti Marsh 51, 96, 97, 103, *118, 119*, 134, 169
Selby's Camp 127
Tsodilo Hills 30, 42, 66, *74, 75*, 153, 155, 181
Tswapong Hills 30
Tuli Block 42, *45*, 94, 96, *106*, 107
Vumbura floodplains *37*
Woodpile Hide 42
Xigera Trail 36, 121, 127
elections 31
elephant-back safaris *40, 120*
elephants *8–9*, 36, *37, 40, 43*, 77, 96, *102–103*, 105, 107, *112*, 118, *120, 128–9, 144*

Ferry crossing *23*
festivals and events
    Desert 1 000: 55
    Ghanzi Agricultural show 55
    Independence Day 49
    Kalahari Summer Festival 49
    Kuru Traditional Dance and Music Festival 55, 65
    October Beer Festival 49
    Sir Seretse Khama Day 55
    Trade Exhibition 55
fires 86, *149, 180*
fishing
    bream 53, 148
    catfish runs 36, 49, 51, 148
    tiger fishing 36, 49, *120*, 121
floodwaters 36, 50, 51, 53, 55, 91, 96, 98, 99, 121, *173*
Francistown 20, 23, 30, 62, 63, 89, 159

Gaborone *10*, 20, 22, 23, 33, 42, 49, 53, 55, 58, 59, 61, 159
    arts and crafts 58
    eating out 58
    nightlife 60
    shopping 58

BOTSWANA The Insider's Guide

Gaborone town plan 70
Gabs–Francistown route 63, 80
game drives 96, 101, 108, 136
Gcwihaba Cave 155
Ghanzi 20, 32, 65, 153, 159
gill nets 148, 149
giraffe 40, 77, 118, 137
Great African Rift Valley 90

High cost–low volume eco-tourism 26
High Court 23
hippo channels 122
history 30–3
HIV/Aids 11, 176, 177
horse safaris 38–9, 121, 126
House of Chiefs 20
huts, mud 12, 13, 16–17

Jao Concession 36, 108, 125
Jwaneng mine 21, 22, 64

Kagiso district 59
Kalahari 32, 42, 55, 62, 66, 89, 90, 124, 181
Kasane–Nata route 76, 77, 118
Kazungula 23, 76 (ferry)
Kgalagadi Transfrontier Park 42, 94, 97, 154
kgosi 168, 189
kgotla 12, 168
Khama111: 32
Khama, Ian 11
Khama, Sir Seretse 11, 32, 33
   plaque at Jwaneng 11
Khutse Game Reserve 94, 154
King's Pool Camp 27, 115
kwaito 82, 189

Lake Ngami 30, 99
languages
   English 176
   Sekalanga 176
   Setswana 10, 20, 176
   Tswana 10, 20
Lepokole Hills 107
Letlhakane mine 21, 22, 80
Letsatse, Intshupeleng 166
Linyanti Concession 27, 96, 97, 124
Linyanti River 8, 30, 36, 49, 51, 53, 93, 103, 124, 133–5, 144
Livingstone, David 32
Livingstone's Baobab 45
London Missionary Society 172

Matuasehube Game Reserve 94, 154
Mahalapye 30, 62
Makgadigkadi Pans 27, 43, 44, 51, 77, 90, 104, 105, 115, 117, 126
markets
   Francistown 63
   Kagiso 59
   Selebi Phikwe–Serule road 156-7
Mashebe, Frank 125

Masire, Dr Ketumile 11, 33
Masoga, Julius 124
Mathambo, Spencer 125
Maun 12, 53, 56, 64, 76, 77, 80, 82–5, 84, 94, 98, 99, 117, 153–4
Maun town plan 71
Moffat, Robert 32
Mogae, Festus 11, 33
mokoro 1, 2, 34–5, 36, 48, 101, 121, 122, 127, 155, 179, 189
Molepolole 30, 32, 154, 159
moloi 180, 189
mopane woodland 8–9, 54–5
morabaraba 61
Moremi Game Park 42, 72, 94, 96, 97, 101, 103, 117, 118, 119
Morupule Colliery Power Station 80
Mothanka, Person 166
mountain bike trails 121
Moutlotse Ruins 107
murals 83, 177
muti 180, 189
Mzilikazi 32

Namibia 66, 89, 144, 148
Nata 16–17, 62, 77
National Assembly 20
Ngotsaa Pan 103
Ntwetwe Pan 105
Nxai Pan National Park 94, 96, 105

Okavango Delta 30, 36, 37, 56, 62, 68, 86–7, 90, 91, 93, 95, 96, 97, 98–100, 114–115, 124, 126, 133, 143, 148
Okavango Delta & Moremi map 72
Okavango options 36–41
Orapa mine 21, 22, 80
Otse Hill 89

Palapye 30, 62, 80
Panhandle 36, 51, 53, 66, 67, 74, 97, 98, 114–115, 117, 121, 131, 179
pans
   Makgadikgadi 27, 43, 44, 45, 51, 77, 90, 104, 105, 115, 117, 126
   Nogotsaa 103
   Ntwetwe 105
   Nxai 96, 105
   Pump 103, 118
   Sua 105
   Tchinga 103
papa 116, 168, 189
Parks, Major 94 (see eco-tourism sites)
   Central Kalahari Game Reserve 94
   Chobe National Park 94
   Kgalagadi Transfrontier Park 94
   Khutse Game Reserve 94
   Mabuasehube Game Reserve 94
   Makgadikgadi Pans 94
   Moremi Game Reserve 94
   Nxai Pan National Park 94
Penman, Mike 124

Planet Baobab 42, 76, 110
plants and trees
   acacia trees 49
   African mangosteen 51
   apple leaf 49
   baobab 45, 49
   bird plum 163
   fireball lily 146
   guarri 163
   indigo dye plant 163
   marula trees 51
   mashatu trees 107
   mopane woodland 8, 54
   papyrus 99
   real fan palm 147
   red star apple 163
   sausage tree 49
   sour plum 51
   umbrella thorns 146
   waterlilies 50, 130
   wild date palm 74, 147
population groups
   Babirwa 30, 166
   Baherero 166, 172
   Bakalanga 30, 166, 176
   Bakgalagadi 30, 64, 166
   Bakgatla 32, 166
   Bakwena 30, 32, 166, 168
   Balete 32
   Bangwaketse 30, 32, 166
   Bangwato 30, 32, 80, 166, 168
   Banoka 166
   Barolong 32, 166
   Basarwa 30, 166
   Basuyiba 30, 159, 166, 168
   Batawana 30, 32, 101, 166, 168
   Batlokwa 32
   Batswana 20, 166, 172, 189
   Batswapong 166
   Bayei 30, 162, 163, 164–5, 166, 179, 180
   Bushmen 27, 30, 43, 64, 65, 66, 82, 107, 168, 181
   Hambukushu 66, 159, 163
   Herero woman 12
   Khoikhoi 30
   !Kung 66, 75
   Mbukushu 30, 166, 172, 179, 180
   Ndebele 32
   Setswana 10, 20
   Sotho 30
   Toutswe 30
   Tswana 10, 20
   Xaniqwee 168
   Zhizo 30
presidents
   Khama, Sir Seretse 11, 32, 33
   Masire, Dr Ketumile 11, 33
   Mogae, Festus 11, 33
Pula 33, 176
Pump Pan 103, 119

Quad biking 44, 104

Radio mast *16–17*
reeds *12, 67, 167*
Rhodes, Cecil John *32, 107*
Riley's garage *84*
River Walk Centre *61*
rivers
    Auob-Nossop *90*
    Boteti *80, 90, 105*
    Chobe *30, 36, 42, 49, 53, 76, 90, 102–103, 117, 133–5, 144, 168*
    Cubango *98*
    Gomoti *98*
    Jao-Boro *98–9*
    Kwando *36, 50, 90, 93, 96, 124, 134–5, 155*
    Kwhai *98, 118*
    Limpopo *30, 90, 105, 107*
    Linyanti *8–9, 30, 36, 49, 51, 53, 93, 103, 124, 133–5, 144*
    Maklautsi *90*
    Maunichira *98*
    Mboroga *98*
    Molopo *90*
    Nata *105*
    Nqoga *98–9*
    Okavango *30, 36, 50, 51, 67, 80, 90, 97–8, 105, 154*
    Quito *98*
    Santantadibe *98*
    Selinda Spillway *90, 93, 99*
    Shashe *62, 107*
    Shasi *90*
    Thamalakane *90, 91, 98–9*
    Thaoge *98*
    Zambezi *23, 90*
roads
    Gabs–Francistown *63, 80*
    Kanye–Gaborone *56–7*
    Kasane–Maun *77, 117*
    Kasane–Nata *76, 77, 118*
    Maun–Chobe *155*
    Maun–Ghanzi *152*
    Moremi–Savuti–Chobe *42*
    Nata–Maun *154*
    Selebi Phikwe *63*
    Shakawe *66*
    Trans-Kalahari Highway *64*
roan antelope *54–5, 97, 103, 135*
Rock Pan *92–3*
Royal Cemetery *81*
Royal route via Serowe *80*
rural village compound *89*

Savuti Channel *92–3, 96, 97, 103*
Savuti Marsh *51, 96, 97, 103, 118, 119, 134, 169*
Sebadietla, Tiny *173*
Sechele *32*
Sehitwa *12*
self-drive *42, 117, 118, 169*
Serowe *30, 80, 81, 159*
Serule *63*
Setlabosha, Ishmael *127*

Shakawe route *66*
Shashe river *62, 107*
Sua Pan *105*
suricates *27, 105*

Tchinga Pan *103*
termites *51, 166*
Thamalakane Bridge *84*
Thapong Visual Arts Centre *158, 159*
Thathaganyana Hill *81*
thunderstorms *46–7, 88, 94*
totems *168*
towns and places
    Aha Hill *155*
    Bethsa *155*
    Bobonong *30, 107*
    D'Kar *55, 64, 65, 159, 177*
    Eretse *155*
    Etsha 13: *163, 166, 173*
    Etsha 6: *66, 163*
    Francistown *20, 23, 30, 62, 63, 89, 159*
    Gaborone *10, 20, 22, 23, 33, 42, 49, 53, 55–6, 58, 59, 61, 159*
    Ganitsuga *155*
    Ghoha Hills *117*
    Gcwihaba Cave *155*
    Ghanzi *20, 32, 65, 153, 159*
    Gumare *66, 159*
    Ihaha *117*
    Jwaneng *21, 22, 64*
    Kachikau *117*
    Kasane *76, 90, 117, 125, 159*
    Kazungula *23*
    Khanye *30, 56, 64, 89, 159*
    Letlhakeng *154*
    Mahalapye *30, 62*
    Maun *12, 53, 56, 64, 76, 77, 80, 82–5, 84, 94, 98, 99, 117, 153, 155*
    Mohembo *98–9*
    Molepolole *30, 32, 154, 159*
    Mombo *97, 109, 116, 124*
    Mopipi *80*
    Nata *16–17, 62, 77*
    Nogatsaa *117*
    Nokaneng *155*
    Nxamaseri *36, 120, 163, 166*
    Palapye *30, 62, 80*
    Pom Pom *121*
    Rakops *80, 154*
    Sehitwa *12*
    Selebi Phikwe *62, 63, 107, 156*
    Sepopa *163*
    Serondella *117*
    Seronga *155*
    Serowe *30, 80, 81, 159*
    Serule *63*
    Shakawe *66, 154*
    Shorobe *117*
    Tchinga *117*
    Thamaga *159*
    Tshabong *154*

    Tshane *154*
    Xai-Xai *155*
    Xudum *121*
traditional fare *82, 116*
traditional healer *172, 180, 189*
Trans-Kalahari Highway *64*
travel advisory *183–8*
Tsodilo Hills *30, 42, 66, 74–5, 153, 155, 181*
Tswapong Hills *30*

United Congregational Church of South Africa *80*

Van der Post panel *74*
Vision 2016 campaign *11*

Wild date palm *74, 147*
wildlife
    aardvark *105*
    brown hyena *97, 105*
    buffalo *77, 97, 103, 142–3*
    caracal *105*
    cheetah *97, 105, 154*
    Chobe bushbuck *103*
    crocodiles *97*
    eland *80, 105, 154*
    elephants *8–9, 36, 37, 40, 43, 77, 96, 102–103, 105, 107, 112, 118, 120, 128–9, 144*
    giraffe *40, 77, 118, 137*
    hippo *103, 122*
    impala *51, 77, 138, 140–1*
    kudu *105*
    leopard *97, 136, 138*
    lions *37, 97, 103, 105, 118, 134*
    oryx *80, 105, 154*
    ostrich *77*
    puku *103*
    red hartebeest *80, 105, 154*
    red lechwe *97, 145*
    rhino *36, 80, 97, 151*
    roan antelope *54, 97, 103, 135*
    sable antelope *42, 77, 97, 103*
    sitatunga *97*
    springbok *80, 154*
    steenbok *77, 138*
    suricates *27, 105*
    tsessebe *51*
    warthog *51, 136*
    wild dogs *42, 96, 125, 139*
    wildebeest *51, 53, 97, 103, 105, 107*
    zebra *51, 53, 77, 80, 97, 103, 105, 107, 123*
wildlife management *26, 150*
Williams, Ruth *32*
witchcraft *180*

Zambezi River *23, 90*
Zambia *30, 89*
Zimbabwe *30, 32, 90, 105, 107*
Zululand *32*

Glossary

Batswana: the collective term for Botswanan citizens (see also 'Motswana')

bogadi: a bride price, which must be paid by the groom's family to the bride's before the marriage can take place

Difaqane: literally meaning 'exodus', this was a period of war in southern Africa when the over-population of fertile land lead to a rise in militancy, especially of the Zulu nation under King Shaka

evapotranspiration: the loss of water from both the ground (through evaporation) and from plants (through transpiration)

kgosi: the village heads or chiefs

kgotla: the traditional village meeting place, where all of the community's social, judicial and political affairs are resolved

kimberlite: a southern African rock formation, in which diamonds are formed

kwaito: a popular southern-African style of dance music

mokolwane: Botswanan name for the real fan palm (*Hyphaene petersiana*)

mokoro (plural *mekoro*): a dugout canoe, traditionally made of wood but today generally made of fibreglass

moloi: a witch or wizard

Motswana: the singular term for a Botswana citizen (see also 'Batswana')

muti: medicine or potion

ngaka: a traditional healer or spirit medium (sometimes called a *sangoma*)

papa: maize porridge

sangoma: see *ngaka*

See also 'So to speak' (pp. 176) for common Setswana terms that you may find useful

---

First published in 2004 by Struik Publishers
(a division of New Holland Publishing (South Africa) (Pty) Ltd)
New Holland Publishing is a member of Johnnic Communications Ltd
Garfield House, 86–88 Edgware Road, London W2 2EA, United Kingdom
www.newhollandpublishers.com
80 McKenzie Street, Cape Town 8001, South Africa www.struik.co.za
3/2 Aquatic Drive, Frenchs Forest, NSW 2086, Australia
218 Lake Road, Northcote, Auckland, New Zealand

Copyright © 2004 in published edition: Struik Publishers
Copyright © 2004 in text: Ian Michler
Copyright © 2004 in photographs: Ian Michler, with the exception of:
p. 7 (bottom right): Corlé Fourie; p. 21: Struik Image Library;
p. 65 (top left): Corlé Fourie; p. 107: Corlé Fourie; p. 111
(far right): Corlé Fourie; p. 121: Corlé Fourie; p. 127 (bottom right):
Corné du Plessis; p. 177 (left): Corlé Fourie
Copyright © 2004 in maps New Holland Publishing (South Africa) (Pty) Ltd

ISBN 1 86872 996 6
1 3 5 7 9 10 8 6 4 2

Publishing manager: Dominique le Roux
Managing editor: Lesley Hay-Whitton
Editor: Monique Whitaker
Senior designer: Alison Day
Cartographer: Sian Marshall
Proofreader: Michelle Coburn
Indexer: Sylvia Grobbelaar

Reproduction by Hirt & Carter Cape (Pty) Ltd
Printed and bound by Sing Cheong Printing Company Limited

All rights reserved. No part of this publication may be reproduced, stored in a retrieval system or transmitted, in any form or by any means, electronic, mechanical, photocopying or otherwise, without the prior written permission of the publishers and copyright holders.

While the author and publisher have made every effort to ensure that the information in this book is correct at the time of going to press, they accept no responsibility for any loss, injury or inconvenience sustained by any person using this book. Please email any comments or updates to: The Editor, BOTSWANA *The Insider's Guide*, updates@struik.co.za